THE REDISCOVERY OF THE HUMAN

Psychological Writings of Viktor E. Frankl
on the Human in the Image of the Divine

THE REDISCOVERY OF THE HUMAN

*Psychological Writings of Viktor E. Frankl
on the Human in the Image of the Divine*

Introduction by Shimon Cowen
Translations by Shimon Cowen and Liesl Kosma

Published by Hybrid Publishers for
The Institute for Judaism and Civilization Inc
Melbourne

HYBRID
PUBLISHERS

Published by Hybrid Publishers for
Institute for Judaism and Civilization Inc,
88 Hotham Street
East St Kilda, Victoria 3183
Australia

Telephone +613 9527 5902

Email: director@ijc.com.au

Introduction and Translations © S. D. Cowen, 2020

This edition first published 2020

NATIONAL
LIBRARY
OF AUSTRALIA

A catalogue record for this
book is available from the
National Library of Australia

ISBN 9781925736656 (p), 9781925736663 (e)

Design & layout by Creative Chinuch
Visit www.creativechinuch.com

Cover design Manfred Cohen
www.bluesquarecreative.com.au

CONTENTS

INTRODUCTION
Shimon Cowen

TRANSLATIONS
*Psychological Writings of Viktor Frankl
on the Human in the Image of the Divine*

PREFACE AND ACKNOWLEDGMENTS

This volume introduces and presents a number of less well-known writings by Viktor Frankl, translated from the original German, in which he forthrightly relates psychology to religious concepts. These cast a strong, new light on the generally received understanding of Frankl's contribution to psychology – "logotherapy". The final sentence of one of these essays, "Ten Theses concerning the 'Person'" is emblematic of their content:

> The true discovery of the human, the *inventio hominis*, occurs in the *imitatio Dei* [the imitation of G-d].

This sentence is remarkable not because it contains any novelty in itself – it expresses a basic notion of millennia of religious teaching and belief. It is remarkable because it was stated by a great psychologist *as a proposition of psychology*. In another of the pieces in this volume, "The Science of the Soul", Frankl writes that psychology is ultimately enclosed within a more comprehensive, theological dimension.

> I like to say that logotherapy is open – and indeed its hallmark is its openness – to a dimension which other schools of psychotherapy are not. This is the theological dimension, which encompasses the anthropological dimension and therefore also psychotherapy (which is within the anthropological dimension)…
>
> Why then do I use the word "dimension"? This word is meant to emphasize not a formal ontological distinction between theology and psychotherapy, but rather what I call a relationship of inclusion. In English, one says: "The higher dimension is the more inclusive one". That is to say, between these individual dimensions, there is not mutual exclusivity, but, to the contrary,

a relationship of inclusion. Put differently, the truth of the one can never contradict the truth of the other (for psychology is situated *within* the wider framework of theology). Indeed, the fact is that only within the higher dimension is the specific reality of the lower dimension illuminated.

The task of the Introduction to these writings of Frankl in this volume is to clarify from the standpoint of this encompassing "dimension" of religious teaching and tradition, acknowledged by Frankl, two aspects of Frankl's work: (1) Frankl's own "logotherapy" with its model of human personality and (2) the seemingly paradoxical goal of Frankl, set out in the Introduction, of a reclamation of the psychotherapy of Sigmund Freud. "Paradoxical", for whilst Frankl's work proceeds from a *rejection* of the fundamental assumptions of Freudian psychoanalysis, he at the same time wanted to *redeem* it for a synthesis with his own Logotherapy.

The teaching of religious tradition, the dimension which, in Frankl's words, is "inclusive" and descriptive of the true nature of the human being, and hence of bearing for psychology, is the tradition from Mount Sinai, which he, as a believing Jew, affirmed. At Sinai, G-d gave both the Ten Commandments, the core of a comprehensive revelation which is the text of the Bible or Pentateuch, the "Written Law, *and* its commentary or elucidation, known as the "Oral Law". Moreover, the tradition from Sinai contains two strands: the laws given to humanity in *general*, known as the Noahide laws, and the laws given *additionally and specifically* to the Jewish people. The former bear the title "Noahide" since those laws were first communicated to humanity in its beginnings and were completed with the survivor of the biblical flood, Noah. The Noahide laws constitute a Divine moral covenant with all of Noah's descendants, that is to say, with humanity at large. Nevertheless, it was the reiteration of the Noahide laws at Sinai which gave them their definitive form and authority. The detail of the Noahide laws, which constitute the shared root of the great world faiths and cultures, is discussed in my book, *The Theory and Practice of Universal Ethics – the Noahide Laws*[1], as in others, and are discussed briefly in the Introduction to this book. Their actuality today is as vital as ever. Even though Frankl himself was Jewish, the Introduction makes it clear that it is this *universal* aspect of the religious tradition from Sinai, the Noahide laws, rather than the additional, specific Jewish laws, which pertain to his psychology.

The psychologist Viktor Frankl was a person of great deed and thought. He

[1] NY: Institute for Judaism and Civilization, 2014.

was not a theologian, although, as noted, he wished to place psychology under the ultimate aegis of theology: "the truth of the one can never contradict the truth of the other". By that criterion we are bound, at the very outset, to point to a contradiction or vicissitude in Frankl's work which expresses itself in relation to a key statement of his in this volume, which we have already quoted: "The true discovery of the human, the *inventio hominis*, occurs in the *imitatio Dei* [the imitation of G-d]". This was removed and a number of fundamental changes made in a later, "modified version" of the "Ten Theses concerning the 'Person'"[2]. It is of the greatest importance here to show why the religious tradition – the higher, "inclusive" dimension – upholds Frankl's first version and rejects his second version. In the following we set out the two versions[3], one after the other, and then analyse the differences, on the basis of which it will be clear that, for the tradition, the first version is the authentic one.

The first version of the ninth and tenth of the "Ten Theses", which appears in this volume, reads as follows:

9. *An animal is not a person* because it cannot elevate itself above itself, or take up a position against itself. That is why the animal does not have the correlate of the person: it has no [morally shaped] world, but only a [conditioning] environment. Extrapolating from the relation animal-human or environment-world, we arrive at the personal G-d and His "worldly" correlate, the "higher world". As the highest spiritual being facing the human being, G-d is at least [spiritual] "person" – in truth, That which is higher than person. All statements about Him could [only] be by way of analogy.

10. *The person is* to be understood finally as *the likeness of G-d*. The human can comprehend him- or herself only from the perspective of transcendence. The human *is* human only insofar as he grasps himself in relation to G-d. He *is* a person only in the measure that he personifies transcendence: tuned and resonant with the summons of transcendence. The summons of transcendence is heard in the conscience. The conscience is the registry of transcendence.

---

[2] The modified version was drawn to my attention by Professor Alexander Batthyány. It was recently republished as an appendage to a new printing of V. Frankl, *Ärztliche Seelsorge – Grundlagen der Logotherapie und Existenzanalyse* (ed. Alexander Batthyány), Vienna: Franz Deuticke, 2005.

[3] The translation of the second version is also that of the present writer.

As little as a human being is what he is in the dimension of immanence [simply being in the world], so little does he [within that perspective] experience what he should be: he is thus unable to "project" *[entwerfen]* and "discover" himself, as an atheistic existentialism imagined he can. The true discovery of the human, the *inventio hominis*, occurs in the *imitatio Dei* [the imitation of G-d].

The revised, second version of the ninth and tenth theses reads:

9. *An animal is not a person* because it cannot elevate itself above itself, or take up a position against itself. That is why the animal does not have the correlate of the person: it has no [morally shaped] world, but only a [conditioning] environment. Extrapolating from the animal-human relation or environment-world, we arrive at a [concept of a] "Supra-world". If we want to characterise the relationship between the (narrow) animal environment to the (wider) world of the person and beyond that to (an all-encompassing) Supra-world, the analogy of the "golden ratio" is useful. [The principle of the "golden ratio"] states that [where a rectangle is divided into a smaller and larger part] the ratio of the smaller part to the larger part, is the same as the ratio of the larger part to the whole [of the rectangle]. Let us take the example of a monkey, which receives painful injections in order to test a serum. Within the horizon of its environment, it is in no position to comprehend the considerations of the human being, who has inserted it into his or her experiment. This is because the human world, the world of meaning and values, is inaccessible to it. It cannot come close to them. It cannot come to this – it does not enter that dimension. Now, are we not compelled to accept that the human world itself, and for its part, is surmounted by a world, which in turn the human cannot access? [Is not that world] with its meaning – its "supra-meaning" – which would alone could make all the human being's suffering meaningful [equally inaccessible to the human]?

Exactly as little as the animal, from the horizon of its environment, can grasp the overarching world of the human, so little can the human grasp the "Supra-world", other than through an intuitive reaching out – though faith. A domesticated animal does not know the purposes to which the human being sets it. How then should the person know what supra-meaning the world as a whole is called to?

10. The person grasps him- or herself only from the standpoint of transcendence. Moreover, one is a person only to the degree that one understands oneself from the standpoint of transcendence. He *is* a person only to the extent that his person is formed by [the standpoint of transcendence]: tuned by, and resonant with, the summons of transcendence. This summons of transcendence finds its reception in the conscience.

For logotherapy, religion is, and can only be, an object, not [its] standpoint. Logotherapy must operate in the practical, innerworldly realm, away from revealed religion. [It must] respond to the question of meaning [practically without posing] an either/or of a theistic and atheistic worldview. When [logotherapy] grasps belief not as belief in G-d, but rather as a comprehensive belief in a meaning, [only] then is it entirely legitimate to concern and occupy itself with belief. Then it agrees with Albert Einstein, who said that to pose the question of the meaning of life is to be religious. [Frankl here inserts a footnote (no. 5): "Religion, vis-à-vis belief in meaning, could ultimately be said to be a radicalisation of the "will to meaning"; specifically inasmuch as it has to do with a "will towards ultimate meaning", indeed, a "will to supra-meaning"].

Meaning is a [boundary] wall, behind which we cannot go – which we much rather need to take on as assumed. We have to accept this ultimate [assumed] meaning, because we cannot question it. The reason we can't is because every attempt to answer the meaning of existence always presupposes the existence of a meaning. In short, the belief in meaning in a person is, in the sense of Kant, a transcendental [–a prior, framing–] category. We know, since Kant, that it is somehow meaningless to question categories like space and time, simply because we do not think – and so cannot question – without already presupposing space and time. Exactly the same applies to human existence: it is always oriented to meaning, however little one may be aware of it. There is always something like a prior sense of meaning and a foreknowledge of meaning and it is the sense of meaning that forms the basis of what logotherapy calls the "will to meaning". Whether one wants it or not, whether one realizes it or not, the human being believes in a meaning as long as one breathes.

Even the suicide believes in a meaning – if not that of life, of living on, then that of dying. If the [suicide] really believed in no meaning, no kind of meaning, he or she would not actually be able to stir a finger to proceed to the act of suicide.

The differences between these two versions are profound. The revised versions of each of ninth and tenth theses are far longer than the original ones. This is necessarily so, for Frankl had to deal with the consequences of their change of stance. Schematically, the differences (with their consequences) between the two versions are as follows: (1) In the first version, Frankl speaks of G-d as an objective reality. In the second, "G-d" is replaced by the term "transcendence" in the sense of an assumed or elected "comprehensive" meaning. In fact, the straightforward language of religious belief in the first version seems in the second to succumb to a scepticism: a person can claim as little knowledge of an ultimate reality (if this is what we call G-d) as an animal has of the world of human purpose and meaning. Religion is simply a *species* of meaning, one characterized by "a will to a Supra-meaning". In the second version, G-d ceases to be absolute. (2) In the first version, the description of the human as spiritually fitted to accomplish the "imitation of G-d" implies an objective, universal ethics, in which that "imitation" consists. In the second version, objective values are replaced by a relativism of meanings. "Religion" has no more significance than asking the meaning of life. Its answer has no priority over any other answer. (3) In the first version, and as brought out by the essays in this volume, "meaning" – worthy of the name – is a *labour* of *self-transcendence*. It is this act of self-transcendence which places the "secular" individual on the same trajectory or route to G-d as the religious person (who has reached its terminus) – even if that person presently considers him- or herself an agnostic or atheist[4]. For self-transcendence leads to that which is rigorously transcendent: G-d. Genuine self-transcendence leads everyone ultimately to the same meaning, the same universal ethics, (the "imitation of G-d") which can

---

[4] See Frankl's explicit rejection of "the bifurcation between atheistic and theistic Weltanschauung" in his "Oskar Pfister Award Lecture" quoted below in Chapter 1 of the Introduction, footnote 30.

be applied and refracted in one's own particular circumstances. In the second version, "meaning" is simply a *fact* (like a Kantian transcendental *a priori*) of human existence. People always *have* – different – meanings and this why, according to this view, a theistic world-view is no more "meaningful" than an atheistic one (which Frankl explicitly rejected in the first version). They are both *immanent* factual descriptions of actually subscribed meanings. (4) In the second version, the scepticism towards the Divine, the moral relativism and the characterization of meaning as "fact" rather than the product of a labour of self-transcendence leads to a validation even of suicide as a "meaningful" act. The writings of Frankl consistent with the first version make it clear that "responsibility" means answering to *life's* demands, to a mission or purpose for *existing*. In the second version, which defines meaning as "factually" held, even the suicide's purported "reason" for suicide is acceptable: one's existence was underlain by a "meaning" which *led* to suicide. The religious tradition, explicitly embraced by the first version, further prohibits suicide as a species of killing because in destroying life (where there is no clear warrant) it destroys Divine property – the Divine likeness stamped in the human being. Indeed, even the great, self-confessedly "religiously tone-deaf" sociologist Max Weber "knew that no redemption religion approves suicide, 'a death which has been hallowed only by philosophies'."[5]

The Viktor Frankl, who authored the essays in this volume, is a believer – *as a psychologist* – in an objective G-d. He believes in objective values and that these morally structure human personality. He maintains that the soul is a reality within the human being and that its unique manifestation is self-transcendence. And he was utterly committed to life, to finding reasons for living, in the most difficult of circumstances.

In response to my query, Professor Alex Batthyány communicated to me that he believes that the revision of the last two theses took place "somewhere in the late 1950s/early 1960s". Indeed, in Frankl's book, *The Will to Meaning*[6], based on lectures given in the United States in 1966, one finds passages which reproduce the language of the revision of the ninth and tenth Theses. There self-transcendence is defined simply as reaching beyond oneself, and to others

---

[5] Preface to the translation by H.H. Gerth and D. Martindale, *Ancient Judaism*, N.Y.: The Free Press, 1952, p. xiii and the quote from Weber comes from *From Max Weber: Essays in Sociology*, tr. by H.H. Gerth and C. Wright Mills, NY: 1946, p. 356.

[6] *The Will to Meaning, Foundations and Applications of Logotherapy*, NY: Plume, 1970.

– people, ideas and things – within the immanent realm of life[7] without any requirement that this self-transcendence transcend towards a transcendental Absolute, Which stands beyond and sets a moral standard *for life*.

In line with the second version of the Ten Theses, in *The Will to Meaning*, Frankl fully acknowledges what he calls the moral "neutralism" of this stance, and also anticipates and answers an obvious challenge to it:

> It follows that a psychotherapist must not impose a value on the patient. The patient must be referred to his own conscience. And if I am asked, as I am time and time again, whether this neutralism would have to be maintained even in the case of Hitler, I answer in the affirmative, because I am convinced that Hitler would never have become what he did unless he had not suppressed within himself the voice of conscience[8].

Here, however, the question must in turn be raised to Frankl's answer: *when* do we say that conscience has been "suppressed" and *what* are our criteria for saying so? The question cannot be answered without an objective (as distinct from a "neutral") framework of values. Frankl continues from the foregoing paragraph:

> It goes without saying that in emergency cases the therapist need not stick to his neutralism. In the face of a suicidal risk it is perfectly legitimate to intervene because only an erroneous conscience will ever command a person to commit suicide. The statement parallels my conviction that only an erroneous conscience will ever command a person to commit homicide, or – once more to refer to Hitler – genocide[9].

Frankl adds that the Hippocratic oath *also* requires the therapist to steer the patient away from suicide, but without this, he here deems suicidal ideation and homicide as products of "erroneous" conscience. The same question arises with regard to "erroneous" conscience as does with his notion of "suppressed" conscience: by what standard is conscience "erroneous"? These questions can be answered only by reference to a universal values framework. What is that framework? The answer of religious tradition and the Frankl of the first version

---

[7] "Human beings are transcending themselves towards meanings which are something other than themselves, which are more than mere expressions of their selves, more than mere projections of these selves", ibid., p. 60.

[8] *Ibid.,* p. 66.

[9] *Ibid.,* pp. 66-67.

of the Theses is that it is the law of the transcendental G-d, Who stated at Mount Sinai "You shall not kill". That is not all that G-d commanded humanity. He also reiterated for humanity a further six Noahide laws, and commanded them to a humanity fashioned with a soul (conscience) capable of resonating with, and through the practical observance of these laws "imitating G-d", should they exercise their free will to do so.

Strangely, having spoken in *The Will to Meaning* of suicide as the product of "erroneous conscience" Frankl, in the same book, again reverts to a "value-neutralism" in regard to suicidal ideation, in words almost identical with the revised version of the tenth Thesis:

> ...it is my contention that man really could not move a limb unless deep down to the foundations of existence, and out of the depths of being, he is imbued by a basic trust in the ultimate meaning. Without it he would have to stop breathing. Even a person who commits suicide must be convinced that suicide makes sense.[10]

Professor Batthyány further communicated to me that, notwithstanding Frankl's revision of the Theses, Frankl "appears to me to gain in spiritual depth, and by no means did he, at that time, disavow...his faith, on the contrary." Indeed, the dialogue, from which "The Science of the Soul", in this volume, is taken, was held in 1984 – well after the second version was written – and yet it expresses the same *pristine religiosity* as the first version of the "Ten Theses". It seems that an ambiguity, arising from the clash of the positions of the first and the second versions of the Ten Theses, continues to run through Frankl's work. This neither disturbs nor deters the undertaking of this volume, which is to present some of Frankl's writings of Frankl, consistent with his first position and with religious tradition, and to seek to elaborate their profound contribution in the Introduction. There are great resources for psychology in this strand of the work of Viktor Frankl, which aligns with, and rests upon, millennia-long religious tradition with its understanding and experience of what the human being is.

Whilst we proceed no further into, nor seek to explain, ambiguity of position in Frankl's work, there is good reason to have mentioned it here, beyond the requirements of scholarly thoroughness. It is that psychology in general, and those following in Frankl's footsteps in particular, need to address the question – which the clash of positions raises – of whether there is an objective

---

[10] *Ibid.*, pp. 150-51.

moral structure to the healthy human personality, and if so, what the source and content of that moral structure is.

This question comes before contemporary psychiatry with new force. Empirical psychology has come to recognize the high positive correlation of mental health and religious belief[11]. This is, moreover, no oddity for some 84% of the world's population is religiously affiliated.[12] And, as we shall see, Frankl argued that the exercise of self-transcendence brings the "atheist" and the "agnostic" also into the realm of spiritual sensitivity. Notwithstanding the acknowledged relevance of religion to human and their mental health, three questions continue to nag at contemporary psychology. (1) Can psychology know whether certain religious beliefs are "healthy" and others "unhealthy", the latter in fact furnishing either or both causes and symptoms of mental illness? (2) Should psychology's stance towards different religious beliefs be relative and neutral? (3) How can therapist and patient, in a therapy which welcomes the spiritual, yet relate to one another over the divide of their different religious-cultural perspectives?

Frankl's thought, as presented in these essays and the Introduction to them in this volume, answers each of these questions. The answer to the first question is that the "healthiness" of religious belief is measured by the extent to which it expresses genuine self-transcendence (as distinct from serving as a veneer for psychophysical or ideological interests); and also in terms of its coherence with literate historical monotheism, as Frankl writes in "Time and Responsibility". Psychologists *as psychologists* may not assess beliefs. That is the province of the "higher, inclusive dimension" – purified, self-transcending religion, situated in literate tradition – which the therapist needs to consult.

The second question, whether psychology should take a wholly neutral, relativistic stand towards the differing beliefs of patients, is prompted by the answer to the first: that *some* beliefs *are* clearly pathological. What then of the rest – should their apparent diversity lead to an attitude of value-neutrality and relativism towards them? We shall see that Gordon Allport in *The Individual and His Religion* sought to practice relativism within a narrow "bandwidth" of what he regarded as "mature religion", as distinct from "authoritarian…

---

[11] See H. G. Koenig et al., *Handbook of Religion and Health,* 2nd Ed'n, Oxford: Oxford University Press, 2012.

[12] Pew Research Center's Forum on Religion & Public Life. 84% of world's population religiously affiliated. Pew Research Center's Forum on Religion & Public Life. See: https://www.pewforum.org/2012/12/18/global-religious-landscape-exec/

immature religion". With this he sought to accommodate a liberal democratic ideal of the individual's – and presumably society's aggregate – freedom to posit values. We see that Allport's limited relativism, expressed in liberal-democratic America in 1949, has seventy years later capsized into full-scale relativism. The moral compass, which he and his contemporaries inherited from religious parents and grandparents and still bounded the scope of acceptable choices, has in many western societies been lost. Not every or any value, which arises from choice, is acceptable. The Viktor Frankl of the essays contained in this volume believed in the objectivity of universal values as rooted in the objectivity and universality of the human soul, the identity and "discovery" of which was to be found in the soul's imitation of G-d.

The third question, how the therapist is to relate to the patient on matters of the spirit across the divide of the particularities of their respective beliefs, is also resolved, as explained in the Introduction, by the coalescence of Frankl's sense of universal values with the Noahide laws. The latter are to be understood as the historical root and resonant common core of the world religions. These values represent the refined common denominator of the world faiths. The differences are particularities. The interaction of the therapist and patient is primarily on this common ground, to which both inherently can come to relate. Consequently, the therapist can obviate the burdensome task of taking a full "spiritual history" of the patient of a different culture, by being versed in this common core of shared human spirituality, without all the cultural particularities. The therapist can readily observe the professional injunctions not to "proselytize" nor to "undermine" the faith of the patient, since both therapist and patient are required to step out of their particular belief frameworks into the domain of a common spirituality. It is sufficient that the therapist be versed in the elements of this common spirituality and be a conduit for the self-transcendence, the spirituality, of the patient. Frankl's work, as presented and elucidated here, shows how spirituality may be applied to psychology: in the logotherapeutic awakening of the human spirit combined with psychotherapeutic healing of personality in accordance with the norms set for heart and mind by the human spirit.

This book combines two monographs previously published by the Institute for Judaism and Civilization. One, fundamentally revised here, was published as *The Human Being in the Image of the Divine: The Psychology of Viktor E. Frankl* (Melbourne: Institute for Judaism and Civilization, 2017). In its new form, it is the Introduction to the section of translations of Frankl's writings. The second, which preceded it, contained four of the five writings of Viktor Frankl included here, and was published as *The Rediscovery of the Human – Basic Early Texts of Viktor E. Frankl* (Melbourne: Institute for Judaism and Civilization, 2014, Second Edition). The "Science of the Soul" has been added here.

The "Introduction" draws substantially on, and in many places reproduces *verbatim* parts of, earlier essays or writings of mine: "Viktor Frankl: Person, Philosopher and Therapist", published in the *Journal of Judaism and Civilization*, Vol. 7 (2005); "Human Personality: The Psychological Matrix of the Noahide Laws" of my *The Theory and Practice of Universal Ethics – the Noahide Laws*, N.Y.: Institute for Judaism and Civilization, 2014; my book-review essay, "Freud and the Mystical Religious Tradition", published in *Journal of Judaism and Civilization*, Vol. 11 (2016); a segment of my contribution to a forum on "The Encounter of Freud and the Fifth Lubavitcher Rebbe", published in the *Journal of Judaism and Civilization*, Vol. 2 (1999); "The Concept of a Person: Reflections on Judaism and Psychotherapy", published in the *Journal of Judaism and Civilization*, Vol. 1 (1998); "Universal Religion, Viktor Frankl and Gordon Allport" in the *Journal of Judaism and Civilization*, Vol. 4 (2002); and "Historical Agreements of Psychology and Religion" published in the *Journal of Judaism and Civilization*, Vol. 10 (2014). All this material is reproduced with permission.

The second part, "Translations" from Frankl's writings have also been previously published. "Time and Responsibility" is my translation of Frankl's short book, *Zeit und Verantwortung* (Vienna: Franz Deuticke Verlag, 1947) which was initially published in the monograph of translations, *The Rediscovery of the Human*, mentioned above. The second writing, "Ten Theses concerning the 'Person'", is a translation of *"Zehn Thesen über die Person"*, included in a short volume of essays by Frankl, entitled *Logos und Existenz* published by Amandus Verlag, Vienna in 1951. The third writing, "Psychological and Pastoral Counselling", is a translation of *"Ärtzliche und priesterliche Seelesorge"*, which appeared in a volume of lectures, originally held by Frankl for radio, entitled *Pathologie des Zeitgeistes – Radiofunkvorträge über Seelenheilkunde* (Vienna: Franz Deuticke Verlag, 1955). The fourth writing, "The Unconditioned Human", translates pp. 52-60 of *Der unbedingte Mensch* (Vienna: Franz Deuticke Verlag, 1949). Here I wish to acknowledge Prof Dr W.J. Maas, who made available to me his abridged translation of this work. The fifth and final writing, translated in this volume as "The Science of the Soul" is a number of selections of Frankl's contributions to a dialogue with Pinchas Lapide, published in their book, *G-ttsuche und Sinnfrage*, Munich: Güterslohe Verlagshaus, 2005. The last four translations were first printed in the *Journal of Judaism and Civilization*, Volumes 3 (2001), 2 (1999) with a different title, 9 (2012), 11 (2016) respectively, and are here reproduced with permission. Rights and permission have been obtained for all the translations. I am the translator of all of these writings except "Medical and Religious Pastoral Care", which was translated by Mrs Liesl Kosma, the late niece of Viktor Frankl.

My initial acquaintance with the work of Viktor Frankl and its importance was due to my friend, Dr Mat Gelman, who has encouraged and assisted me throughout with both research into, and dissemination of, the work of Viktor Frankl. The work of translation gave me an intimate sense of the spirit of Frankl's work. Mrs Liesl Kosma, who lived in Melbourne, facilitated my exposure to some important early German works of Frankl. In most of my translations of Frankl's work, a colleague, Dr Chris Wurm, has been a generous and highly expert reader and reviewer, who thereby helped to fine-tune my understanding of Frankl in general. My wife Miriam, as in virtually all my work, has striven, where she had the opportunity, to make my writing clearer.

Finally, I would like to express my gratitude to the family of Viktor Frankl, Mrs Elly Frankl, Viktor Frankl's widow, and Frankl's son-in-law, Professor Franz Vesely, and a close friend of the Frankl family and worker for the Viktor Frankl Institut in Vienna, Professor Alex Batthyány, for their kind assistance over many years.

Rabbi Dr Shimon Cowen,
Director, Institute for Judaism and Civilization

INTRODUCTION

CHAPTER 1

VIKTOR FRANKL: PERSON, PHILOSOPHER AND THERAPIST

The "living example" of self-transcendence

One of the great spiritual leaders of modern times, Rabbi Menachem Mendel Schneerson, known as the Lubavitcher Rebbe, wondered in a letter written in 1969[1], at the failure of Viktor Frankl's teachings to gain wider dissemination in therapeutic practice. The question presumably arose because of the deep congruence of Frankl's thought with millennia of religious tradition and yet its failure to win wider acceptance. An answer which Rabbi Schneerson gave, though it did not satisfy him entirely, was that it had to do with the lack of therapists displaying "the living example" required for the practice of "logotherapy", the name Frankl gave to his unique contribution to psychology. To arouse the spiritual essence of the human being, in its primary quality of self-transcendence, as logotherapy seeks to do, the therapist must him- or herself manifest the quality of self-transcendence.

Viktor Frankl's theory is about the human being's need for meaning and the importance of the role of meaning in psychological wellbeing. It is, however, according to the strand in Frankl's thought, which his writings in this volume illustrate, crucially more than that: it is not about *any* meaning. It is about the ultimate and objective or universal meanings to which the trajectory of self-transcendence leads. Self-transcendence, Frankl wrote, puts even the secular individual – and even the self-perceived "atheist" or "agnostic" – on a route, the end-station of which the religious person has already reached. The secularist may call this agency of self-transcendence "conscience"; the religious person is able to call it by its exact name: the soul. The soul draws towards

---

[1] Rabbi Menachem Mendel Schneerson, *Igros Kodesh*, NY: Kehos, Vol 25, Letter No. 9,622 (3 Tamuz, 5729), pp. 301-02.

its source, G-d, Whom it seeks to "imitate". As discussed in the Preface, the core statement of this idea, not novel in itself from a religious point of view, but powerful because a great *psychologist said it, as a psychologist*, is found in the tenth of Frankl's "Ten Theses concerning the 'Person'", translated in this volume, which we yet again quote:

> The true discovery of the human, the *inventio hominis*, occurs in the *imitatio Dei* [the soul's imitation of G-d].

The essential will of the soul is to bring the human "self", which houses it, to living out the ethical and meaningful responses to life's circumstances, into which the "imitation" of G-d translates. In the sentence just quoted, through self-transcendence the person makes the "true discovery" of him- or herself. Frankl's own journey towards "logotherapy" required *him* to become, in the words of the Lubavitcher Rebbe, a "living example" of self-transcendence. This came by stages and trials.

The first articulate intellectual phase of Frankl's life – his precocious later high school and early tertiary student years – embraced a concept of the human being, which Frankl later came to reject. This concept went together with his early adherence to the teachings of Sigmund Freud[2], which he would subsequently represent as a "reductionist" view of the human being. This reductionism consisted in a view that "reduced" human personality to an instinctual base, primarily in physical drives (the *Id*), and studied the dynamics of their fulfilment or repression. According to this view, "mind" (the *Ego*) was, according to Frankl's reading of Freud, itself "secondarily" derived from physical drives.[3] As for the third faculty of human personality, to which conscience or soul lays claim, Freud saw this as no more than an oppressive fiction, a social and historical *Super-ego*, instructing the Ego to repress the Id's desires in the interests of "morality". Freud dismissed any claim to truth for belief in G-d, religion or the human soul – all traditional content of the Super-ego. The adolescent and young adult Frankl could go along with Freud, since, as he wrote, "As a child I was religious, but during puberty I passed through an atheistic phase."[4]

---

[2] He also communicated with Freud, sending him a paper which Freud at once forwarded for publication to the *International Journal of Psychoanalysis*. See Viktor Frankl, *Recollections – An Autobiography*, trans Joseph and Judith Fabry, NY: Plenum Press, 1997, p. 48.

[3] For Freud, "Even that 'jurisdiction' in the person which comes forth against these urges – whether to suppress, censure or to sublimate them – is itself functionally derived from drives, recoupled with drives. In other words, behaviour which does not simply *consist* of urges, at least derives from them." "Psychological and Pastoral Care" (in this volume).

[4] *Recollections*, p. 57.

Freud's species of reductionism, based on the primacy of physical instinct, the repression of which accounted for neurosis, eventually palled for Frankl. This disillusionment with Freud came finally when Frankl applied formally for membership of Freud's association, the Vienna Psychoanalytic Society. For this purpose, he met with Freud's associate Paul Federn, who routinely questioned him, "And what about your neurosis?"[5]

After detaching himself from Freud, Frankl wandered to another species of reductionism, that of Alfred Adler. Adler, also a former, disaffected student of Freud, had established a school of "individual psychology", construing personality in terms of complexes relating to issues of power in society. As Frankl would later acknowledge, in its reduced vision of the human (that also discounted any role for the autonomous human spirit or conscience), "sociologism" merely substituted for the "psychologism" of Freud. There was a "nihilism" implicit in both these truncated views of the human being – the term "nihilism", as Frankl later explained it, signifying essentially "nothing other than" the lower bases, to which these doctrines reduced the human being. He would later see in nihilism – in its dismissal of ultimate, objective values – a philosophical and cultural foundation for the holocaust[6].

Frankl's intellectual departure – facilitated by expulsion – from the circle of Adler, completed his rejection of reductionism and was accompanied by the recovery of the religious belief of his childhood. Frankl had been born to parents of strong Jewish belief. In his *Recollections* he speaks of his mother as "deeply pious"[7] and of his father as stern but just[8], with a strong professed faith even under the extreme conditions of his deportation to the death camps[9].

---

[5] As quoted from an interview with Frankl in H. Klingberg Jr, *When Life calls out to Us – The Love and Lifework of Viktor and Elly Frankl*, NY: Doubleday, 2001, p. 53. Frankl states that he thereafter went to a park, where he sat down and pondered, "What kind of a science is psychoanalysis if you can't judge it on rational grounds, but you have to be indoctrinated first before you can agree with it?" (quoted, *ibid.*).

[6] As Frankl wrote in his *Recollections*, "I am absolutely convinced that the gas chambers of Auschwitz, Treblinka, and Majdanek were ultimately prepared not in some Ministry or other in Berlin, but rather at the desks and in the lecture halls of nihilistic scientists and philosophers", p. 49.

[7] *Recollections*, p. 9.

[8] *Ibid.*, p. 22. The family kept the Jewish dietary laws, Frankl recalls, up to the First World War, and that his father was once called to the Government Ministry, in which he worked, on the Day of Atonement and (in accordance with the laws of that day) refused to write, even though he was disciplined for this.

[9] *Ibid.*, p. 26.

Frankl's father prayed regularly with the phylacteries *(tefillin)* containing sections of the Scripture relating to the unity of G-d, worn on the arm against the heart and on the head against the brain, by the traditional Jew; and so too would Frankl regularly don *tefillin* after the war. This was an informed, spiritually literate religious background with which Frankl could reconnect.

The German word *Geist* was amongst those used by Frankl to refer to the highest faculty of the human being. It translates into English as "spirit" – as distinct from "mind", which is the authentic translation of the German word, *Seele*. It is the meaning-seeking and positing faculty in the human being and Frankl turned increasingly towards it. During the interwar years, starting in 1923, Frankl developed not only his critique of reductionist psychology, but also aspects of the theory and methodology of logotherapy, a therapy focused on "logos" or meaning. Thus, he stated that in 1929 he had already developed his concept of three possible ways of a person's finding meaning: in "1) a deed we do, a work we create; 2) an experience, a human encounter, a love; and 3) when confronted with an unchangeable fate (such as an incurable disease), a change of attitude toward that fate."[10] From 1933 on, he used the term *Existenzanalyse* ("existential analysis" or the "analysis of [personal] existence") for the philosophical tool of logotherapy (which we discuss in the next section), and had to some extent formulated his mature ideas[11]. His therapeutic method of "paradoxical intention", employed in logotherapy, was also developed at this time[12].

This post-reductionist, middle phase of Frankl's thought witnessed the German *Anschluss* – annexation and Nazification – of Austria in 1938 and sees him at work in conditions of extraordinary exigency. Suffering the indignities of the everyday degradation and persecution of the as yet undeported Jewish citizens of Vienna, he was still allowed to continue to work in a Jewish psychiatric hospital, where his principal efforts were directed to countering the tide of suicide amongst Jews living in that utterly dark and sad time. He also protected a number of patients from Nazi "mercy killing" of the mentally ill, through changing their diagnoses and locations[13]. In 1941 he married his first wife, Tilly Grosser, whom he lost in the concentration camps.

---

[10] *Ibid.*, p. 64.

[11] *Ibid.*

[12] *Ibid.*, p. 73. See the final section of Chapter 2 of this Introduction.

[13] As pointed out in M. Gelman *et. al.*, "Viktor Emil Frankl", *American Journal of Psychiatry* 157:4, April 2000, p. 625. This is detailed by Frankl in "The Science of the Soul".

In the interwar years, notwithstanding his devoted work in the psychiatric hospital, Frankl was less than ascetic[14]. With all his humanity and dedication, his was not yet a life lived wholly under the aegis of conscience and transcendent spiritual conviction. This would come in the next phase.

The crystallization of Frankl's character as the "living example" of self-transcendence, required for logotherapy, came in what he called the "crucial experiment" of the concentration camps, following his deportation in 1942. A famous story, told by Frankl of himself as a concentration camp inmate, brings out this completion of character. It is a story of an assembly of inmates, Frankl among them, who were stripped of their clothing and given those of other, murdered inmates. When Frankl was stripped of his clothing including a coat, into the lining of which he had sewn the notes for the book, *The Doctor and the Soul*, he momentarily entertained suicidal thoughts. The goal of publication of this book had been the purpose and hope, which at that time sustained him in life.

> Thus, I had to overcome the loss of my spiritual child, as it were, and had to face the question of whether this loss did not make my life void of meaning. An answer to this question was given to me soon. In exchange for my clothes, I was given the rags of an inmate who had already been sent to the gas chamber; in a pocket I found a single page torn from a Hebrew prayer book. It contained the main Jewish prayer, *Shema Yisrael*, i.e. the command 'Love thy G-d with all thy heart, and with all thy soul and with all thy might', or as one could interpret it as well, the command to say 'yes' to life despite whatever one has to face, be it suffering or even dying. A life, I told myself, whose meaning stands or falls on whether one can publish a manuscript would, ultimately, not be worth living. Thus, in that single page which replaced the many pages of my manuscript I saw a symbolic call henceforth to live my thoughts instead of merely putting them on paper.[15]

This passage sets forth the central tenet of self-transcendence: that life has not to do with what *I* want of life, with my present perceived interests, but with what *life* wants of me. I open myself to "that" which is beyond "me", and

---

[14] See H. Klingberg, *op. cit.*, p. 81.

[15] Frankl, *Psychotherapy and existentialism*, NY: Washington Square Press, 1967, pp. 25-26. Cited by Klingberg, p. 132-3.

thereby discover or actualize my essential self.

Freed from the camps, Frankl returned to Vienna, and to his clinical work. He met Elly Shwindt[16], whom he married upon formal notification of the death of his first wife, Tilly. Continuing as Director (a position he had originally assumed in 1946) of the neurology section of the *Poliklinik* Hospital in Vienna, he then embarked with her assistance upon the world-wide dissemination of the teaching of logotherapy: through millions of miles of lecture touring, the treatment or comfort given to thousands of patients in therapeutic practice and his prolific writing.

The analysis of personal existence

The framework of personal existence

Frankl writes in his *Recollections* that, as he progressed towards the mature formulation of his ideas, he struggled philosophically with the cultural experience of meaninglessness – the "sickness of the age", as he called it. He sought to address the contemporary philosophical sense of the dismemberment of existence, expressed in "transitoriness". Thus, Frankl writes, as a child, "one evening just before falling asleep, I was startled by the unexpected thought that one day I too would have to die. What troubled me then – as it has done throughout my life – was not the fear of dying, but rather the question of whether the transitory nature of life might destroy its meaning."[17] The very same question was raised by contemporaneous "existentialist" philosophy. This philosophy, however, responded not through questing meaning, but rather by heightening and affirming a sense of objective meaninglessness. To this existentialism, Frankl counterposed his own *Existenzanalyse*, the "analysis of [personal] existence", which, to the contrary, grasped time – the history of an individual's life – as the repository of cumulative, enduring personal "actualizations" of value.

Much of Frankl's essay, "Time and Responsibility", in this volume, addresses this theme. Briefly, he enunciates the concept that everything a person does is in fact stored-up within the past, and as such lives forward into the present and the future. This means, on the one hand, that all the good that one has done in one's lifetime (until the present) cannot be taken away from one. It is

---

[16] Elly, unlike Frankl's first wife, Tilly Grosser, was not Jewish, but she respected Viktor's traditional Jewish practices. On a visit to Vienna, I was shown by Elly Frankl the *tefillin* and the *talis koton*, which he would wear during his prayers.

[17] *Recollections*, p. 29.

an eternal accomplishment. As for the not-good of one's past, the present offers the constant opportunity for a change of course and the accomplishment of new good. To the contrary, the not-good of the past may be partially redeemed inasmuch as the consciousness and regret of it acts as a spur to actualization of the "second chance" offered by the present. Thus, Frankl's "categorical imperative" is to "act as though you have a second chance at life, and the first time around did as badly as you possibly could have"[18].

Curiously, Frankl does not provide a philosophical or metaphysical explanation of *why* the past – lived actualization and achievement – is "held" and carried forward into the future. From the standpoint of religious tradition, however, one could supply two aspects of the answer to this question. The "world" is a spatio-temporal *whole* before its Creator, Who recreates and sustains it in all its spatio-temporal moments, and Who "remembers" them all. Significantly, the existentialist philosophy of his contemporaries, which Frankl rejects, comprehends time as distinct particles, with no inherent continuity, because it has no sense of a Creator, Who both engenders and binds them together. All that is left for this existentialism is mere, discontinuous transience of time and things – a fractured immanence, "transitoriness". On the other hand, Frankl's existential analysis employs a transcendental perspective, which envelopes time and space, "holds" and gathers up everything which occurs within it *sub species aeternitatis* ("beneath the gaze of eternity"). Or, to use another expression of Frankl, the transcendent Divine is the "coordinate system" itself[19]: the past, present and future, from this perspective, coexist, and are a whole, before G-d.

The second basis for the continuity and preserved history of a human life is to be found for Frankl in the essential personhood of the human being – the soul. Frankl states that the relationship of the soul to mind and body is that

---

[18] *"Die Existenzanalyse und die Probleme der Zeit"*, in *Logos und Existenz* (Vienna: Amandus Verlag, 1951), p. 39-40. The notion that one can change course parallels the religious concept of repentance, which alters one's "verdict" before G-d from "now on". The further concept of a profounder repentance which can reach back "into the past" and actually "alter" it, may not be relevant here. See Rabbi M. M. Schneerson, *Likkutei Sichos* (NY: Kehot), Vol. 6, pp. 46-56.

[19] See "Time and Responsibility", below p. 116. This is similar to the religious concept, G-d "is the place of the world, and the world is not His place" (*Yalqut Shimoni Vayetze remez* 117). Frankl uses a term of Hegel – *aufbewährt* (similar to *aufgehoben* [taken up]) – which means "preserved". Hegel's metaphysic is also one of the unity of being, but different from Frankl's. Hegel's view is more a pantheistic one, which sees being and G-d as coextensive, whilst Frankl grasps the transcendence of G-d.

the soul has mind and body as its vehicles. It is their higher and collective identity. Precisely the soul is the continuous identity of the human being through all the moments of the person's life. Not only does life not fragment the identity of the soul; so, also, death does not disturb it. Hence, he writes, death is not a prospect of annihilation which awaits the person. Rather, in death, the person, who hitherto was a soul, which *also had* body and mind, now upon losing body and mind *becomes* wholly the soul. The soul of the human being is the locus of continuous identity of the human being, the "I" which possesses a cumulative history. Hence, Frankl can state that we write "the logbook of the world"[20]: our individual lives are continuities, strands of world-history. The "world" has continuous identity under the auspices of the transcendent Divine and Divine Providence; and the "person" has continuous identity under the auspices of the soul.

Freedom and responsibility

In contradistinction to the reductionism of Freud, in which the human being is grasped as *driven* by physical instinct, Frankl states in *"Die Existenzanalyse und die Probleme der Zeit"*, "It is certainly true that the Id drives, but it is thereby forgotten, that the 'I' wants, that the 'I' – decides!"[21] To be "driven" by instinct is to choose to allow oneself to be so driven[22]. Existence is not conditioning being, being which can be in no other way, a "so" (*So-sein*) – but rather *being there for* (*Da-sein*) a purpose to be actualized. It is an existence which "can become something else" *(Anders-werden-können)*[23].

Finally, it is important to understand the context in which freedom and responsibility work within the human personality. Of course, whilst the psychophysical dimensions do not exclusively determine human conduct, at the same time, they are a factor – they may limit possibilities. Yet, at the same time their influences exist alongside the exercise of conscious moral choice. Frankl speaks of the relationship between the levels within the human being, body, mind and soul: that "the physical makes possible the mental realization of a spiritual demand."[24] The formula is a profound one. One must work within one's physical constitution and possibilities as a particular human being. It is

---

[20] "Time and Responsibility", below p. 98.

[21] *"Die Existenzanalyse und die Probleme der Zeit"*, p. 38.

[22] *Ibid.*, pp. 34-35.

[23] *Ibid.*, p. 38.

[24] "The Unconditioned Human", below p. 153

mind, which has the ability to mobilize that body to a particular stance in the moment and in the world. But that *to which* the mind orders and mobilizes the physical must be according to the mandate of conscience. Frankl employs a beautiful metaphor:

> the spiritual person relates to his or her organism analogously to the way a musician relates to the musical instrument. A sonata cannot be played without a piano and a pianist. This analogy explains something – virtually everything. But just as every analogy is lacking in some respect, so too this one: one can see the pianist, whilst the soul is essentially invisible…the pianist and the piano stand on the same level… whilst the soul and the body by no means stand on one and the same ontological level[25].

Freedom exists because the human being is *not* solely driven by physical and psychological dimensions of personality. The person also possesses a soul, with *its* decisions as to how physical and psychological demands should be adjudicated and how the psychophysical dimensions should serve the soul's projects. Out of the potential or real conflicts of soul and psychophysical self, human freedom and choice emerges as to which will be master. For the soul, this exercise of freedom is paired with responsibility: in Frankl's words, human *freedom* is *"an analysis of the human in the light of responsibility."*[26] Freedom cannot be only freedom "from"; it must also be freedom "to"[27]. For Frankl, this concept of the responsible exercise of freedom, however, also relates to the question of the *nature of the values*, which this freedom should be utilized to access and to actualize.

The objectivity of values

Frankl is quoted by Elisabeth Lukas as stating that "logotherapy is not neutral as to values."[28] A basic feature of Frankl's thought (and certainly of the essays contained in this volume) is the universal validity of the values promulgated to all humanity from Mt Sinai. Whilst Frankl took it as a psychotherapeutic principle not to impose belief upon patients, this was pre-eminently because it was psychotherapeutically unproductive. Any constitution of meaning on the part of a patient had necessarily to be one accomplished by the patient for

---

[25] *Der Unbedingte Mensch – Metaklinische Vorlesungen*, p. 53.

[26] *"Die Existenzanalyse und die Probleme der Zeit"*, p. 33

[27] *Ibid.*

[28] E. Lukas, *Logotherapy Textbook* (transl. T. Brugger), Toronto: Liberty Press, 2000, p. 61.

it to be authentically *meaningful* and therapeutically effective for the patient. The task of the therapist was to prompt self-transcendence, the vehicle of the discovery of values and meaning.

Notwithstanding this, he saw universal values of conscience and upheld the concept that the person's modelling of the Divine as the truest and deepest *discovery* of this essential self. The connection between the two, as explained by religious tradition and set out at length in the next chapter, is that the modelling of the Divine – that is, of Divine attributes – translates into universal rules of concrete ethical conduct. Self-transcendence is the awakening of the soul itself, and everyone has one, whether expressed or repressed or in some intermediate degree. Hence, every genuine act of self-transcendence even on the part of the "non-religious", indeed also the self-professed "atheistic", person awakens the soul and sets one *en route* to the "end station" of conscious belief in G-d[29]. Just as self-transcendence leads to G-d, so does it lead to the Divinely prescribed values, in which the "imitation of G-d" consists. The meanings to which logotherapy can help the "agnostic" or "atheist"[30] and the conscious believer alike reveal themselves as applications of these universal values[31] to

---

[29] See "Time and Responsibility", below pp. 109-10, 112-13; "The Science of the Soul", below pp. 134-36

[30] "G-d is the partner of our most intimate soliloquies. That is to say, whenever you are talking to yourself in utmost sincerity and ultimate solitude – He to Whom you are addressing yourself may justifiably be called G-d. As you notice, such a definition circumvents the bifurcation between atheistic and theistic *Weltanschauung* [world-view]. The difference between them emerges only later on, when the irreligious person insists that his soliloquies are just that, monologues with himself, and the religious person interprets his as real dialogues with someone other than himself. Well, I think that what here should count first and more than anything else is the 'utmost sincerity' and honesty. And I am sure that if G-d really exists he certainly is not going to argue with the irreligious persons because they mistake Him for their own selves and therefore misname Him", "Oskar Pfister Award Lecture", appended to the text of the *The Unconcious G-d*, to produce a new book, *Man's Search for Ultimate Meaning* (NY: Plenum Press, 1997), p. 151.

[31] "First of all there are meaning-universals *[Sinnuniversalien]*...That is, there are the Ten Commandments...values, which have been crystallized in the course of human history and across human society...Values are general guidelines of action...The meaning, of which logotherapy speaks is not universal meaning, but rather unique meaning, of which logotherapy as non-religion, non-pastoral activity may speak and can speak with every patient... I have interpreted the conscience as that organ which allows the [human being] to find the specific and unique meaning of any situation" "Gespräch mit Wolfram Kurz und Viktor Frankl" in M Seidel (ed.), *Die Kunst, sinvoll zu leben*, Tübingen: Verlag Lebenskunst, 1996, pp. 23-24 (present writer's translation).. "Unique meanings" appear as applications of "general meanings", as we see in "The Science of the Soul" (below p.

the particular situation or predicament of the individual.

As a step towards self-transcendence comes Frankl's employment of logo-therapy, in his own words, to *relativize the relative*. That means, to show a patient that a perspective, interest or predicament in which one is immured, is being asserted from a personal, "localized" viewpoint. It is what "I" want or feel here and now, and that needs to be relativized to the bigger perspective of what *life* wants of me.

The "existentialist" philosophies of Sartre and Heidegger – to which Frankl opposed his "existential analysis" – because they remained without transcendent moral reference could and in fact did lead their authors to moral lapse: Heidegger, in a moment, to endorse Hitler and National Socialism, and Sartre, in a moment, to endorse Stalin at the height of his terror. Their recantations do not diminish the hazardousness of their removal of a transcendent moral compass. The existential analysis of Frankl, on the other hand, is associated with a universal and objective moral compass, as integral to, and constitutive of, being human[32].

The logotherapeutic intervention

The levels of the "layered" structure of human personality –body, mind and the noetic (or meaning) faculty – may join in various combinations or interact to produce a particular psychological disorder[33]. On their own levels, however, they can present in the patient qualitatively different kinds of psychological disorder. A (purely) existential crisis manifests within the noetic consciousness

---

142), that Frankl sees individual situations with their meaning-content as *applications* of universal moral commandments to the specificity of the moment (below p. 136). It is actually more accurate to state, as noted, that the Noahide – rather than the Ten – commandments are the truly universal biblical commandments for all humanity. See the next chapter for a comprehensive discussion of this.

[32] *Die Existenzanalyse und die Probleme der Zeit, op cit.,* p. 41. Elisabeth Lukas *(loc. cit.)* wrote that conscience consists of universal values which at some level human beings commonly intuit. We shall, in the next chapter, present these universal values, as expressed in the Noahide laws. Frankl's actual adherence to these values is documented in S.D. Cowen, "Viktor Frankl's logotherapy and universal values", *The International Forum for Logotherapy,* 28:1, Spring 2005, pp. 47-54.

[33] In the words of James Dubois, the translator of Frankl's *Theory and Therapy of Mental Disorders* in his Introduction to the translation, "In fact there are no purely somatogenic, psychogenic, or noogenic neuroses, but rather only mixed cases – cases in which a somatogenic, psychogenic, or noogenic aspect pushes into the foreground of the theoretical or therapeutic field of vision (Translator's Introduction to *On the Theory and Therapy of Mental Disorders,* N.Y.: Brunner- Routledge, 2004, p. xlv).

of a person who may be mentally and somatically healthy. A neurosis characteristically inhabits the realm of the *mental*, perceptual realm of psyche, whilst psychosis relates to the physical, organic or somatic – the *bodily* – level of psyche. Alternatively, the "one" presenting psychological disorder could originate (–be caused–) primarily at different levels of personality and so owe its real differences to those different levels. Logotherapeutic intervention functions differently and has different scope at these different levels.

Thus, a psychological disorder must first be located at its primary level of origin. Often, Frankl would here employ the analogy of the same "circle", which can equally represent the base of a cone, a ball or a two-dimensional circle – all quite *different* objects. Similarly, as mentioned, the "one" symptomatic, presenting condition must be examined for its primary source in personality. Thus, depression, for example, can be of a clinical-somatic character; it could be neurotic in the mental-perceptual dimension; or it could be the expression of an "existential despair" at the meaning or noetic level. The failure to recognize the level of the malaise can thwart therapy or worse. Rational discourse, often employed by logotherapy, addressed to a psychotic condition can be futile. Conversely, to treat what is essentially a crisis of meaning in the noetic faculty solely with chemical tranquillizers instead of taking a logotherapeutic approach is only to suppress the crisis and mistake its source. Whilst Frankl's logotherapy, with its "existential analysis" is entirely appropriate to disorders within the noetic realm, psychological disorders with somatic or mental causes will call for psychotherapies germane to those levels of personality in addition to any appropriate logotherapeutic intervention. Nevertheless, even at these levels there may be a vital role for logotherapeutic intervention, which seeks to leverage the resources of the healthy spirit wherever it can manifest itself.[34] The soul or spirit identifies and is then brought to bear upon what is not it: illness. It has distinct roles and interventions in psychosis, neurosis and noetic crisis.

Psychotic illness is, as mentioned, the least amenable to a spiritual or meaning-intervention. Nevertheless, the residue of the spiritual consciousness (which in itself never becomes sick) within a particular psychotic individual *can* and must

---

[34] Thus, Lukas writes, "Since logotherapy's particular attention is the best possible means of dealing with psychic dysfunctions and not the search for causes, it is rather a 'discovering' psychotherapy and not an 'uncovering' one. What it seeks to discover are the healthy and intact sources in human beings 'in their exact equivalence' which are inclined toward the logos [i.e. ethical meaning]" (*op. cit.*, 86-87).

be summoned[35]. Thus, Frankl writes of the patient with schizophrenia, the somatic (physical) mental illness *par excellence*[36] – in which mind can lose its function as an active *subject* (becoming the passive *object*, a hearer of voices) –

> …even for the schizophrenic there remains that residue of freedom towards fate and toward the disease, which man always possesses, no matter how ill he may be, in all situations and at every moment of life, to the very last[37].

In the *Doctor and the Soul* Frankl wrote, "psychosis is at bottom a kind of test of a human being, of the humanity of a psychotic patient"[38], a test presumably which the patient, with his or her residual *human* spirit, can yet in some way pass.

Frankl states that neuroses invariably have not just mental but also a factor of physiological or somatic causation[39]. These might be constitutional – hereditary dispositions – or conditional upon experiences such as childhood trauma or neglect or severe illness. Logotherapy and existential analysis (the practical-philosophical tool of logotherapy) have "no foothold … in the physiological bases of neurosis"[40]. Yet, in neurosis there is a moment of decision (however conscious or unconscious) by which the patient takes this physiological-somatic basis and *builds* an actual neurosis out of it[41]. And just as it was decision that

---

[35] One must communicate and evoke the healthy element within, refraining from pathologizing it. Hence, "Logotherapy declares war on pathologism. As I have said, two times two make four, even if a paranoid patient says it." *Recollections*, p. 75.

[36] "In schizophrenia, then, the person's integral humanity is affected by the psychotic process…As such, as a true disease 'of the mind,' schizophrenia – in contrast to obsessional neurosis – is a 'creatural affliction.'" *The Doctor and the Soul*, pp. 256-57.

[37] *Ibid.*, p. 257. Thus, Frankl spoke of "our psychiatric credo: this unconditional faith in the personal spirit – this 'blind' faith in the 'invisible' but indestructible spiritual person! If I, Ladies and Gentlemen, did not have this belief, I would rather not be a doctor" Der Unbedingte Mentsch, p. 57 (present writer's translation)..

[38] Further, in *The Doctor and the Soul*: "Endogenous psychoses are also susceptible to treatment by logotherapy: not the constitutional components themselves, of course, but the psychogenetic components resulting from them…to change the patient's attitude towards her disease as well as her life as a task" (p. 239). Similarly, "The organic condition underlying psychosis is always transposed into the properly human sphere before it becomes the psychotic experience; the organic condition must be used humanly" (p. 242).

[39] "It is highly probable that no genuine neurosis in the clinical sense has arisen entirely without a constitutional – that is, an ultimately biological – underlying cause" *ibid.*, p. 203.

[40] *Ibid.*, p. 202.

[41] "At one time in life every psychopath stands at the crossroads where he must decide

developed neurosis, so may the same power of decision be invoked to respond to it and to help throw it off: "existential analysis aims to bring the person to an understanding of his true life task, for with such understanding he will find it all the easier to cast off his neurosis."[42]

Frankl writes that "The human – and *precisely the neurotic* – has no greater need than to be as aware as possible of his or her own responsibility."[43] For if the psychotic – bodily – level of personality cannot *itself* listen to its highest self's (the soul's) presentation of meaning, the mental level *can*. Frankl cites Ludwig Klages' phrase of *"Geist als Widersache der Seele"* ("the spirit as *counterweight* to the mental [the potentially neurotic] realm.")[44] Thus, P. Polak writes that logotherapy can help the patient to grasp neurosis as a possible but falsely chosen or accepted "potential of being" (*Seinkönnen*), and cause "neurosis to be seen as the expression of a spiritual crisis [that is, a bad decision]."[45] The patient is to grasp that the neurosis opposes his or her essential self. The compulsion which the neurotic experiences, must be comprehended by him as something "that he 'has', but is not 'he himself'"[46]. The neurotic must know him or herself as free to "accept or reject the promptings of impulse"[47].

The twin logotherapeutic methods of self-distancing and self-transcendence are applicable to neurosis. Thus, in the case of sexual neuroses (such as impotence), dereflection (a form of self-distancing) is stressed at the very same time as the transcendent ideal of focus on the other as an object of genuine love and care, rather than upon sexual performance[48].

In regard to crises of a noetic or meaning character, Frankl writes at the beginning of "Psychological and Pastoral Care" that ever increasingly people come to the psychotherapist instead of the religious mentor, though they come for the same guidance. That is, they come with existential issues or from an existential crisis. In such circumstances, the application of psychological

---

between the mere disposition and its elaboration into actual psychopathy" *ibid.*, p. 218. See Frankl's discussion of this process in the case of an obsessional neurosis *(ibid)*.

[42] *Ibid*, p. 203

[43] "Time and Responsibility", below p. 91. Emphasis added.

[44] *Der Unbedingte Mensch*, p. 19.

[45] *Frankls Existenzanalyse in ihrer Bedeutung für Anthropologie und Psychotherapie*, Innsbruck-Wien: Tyrolia-Verlag, 1949, p. 11.

[46] *Doctor and the Soul*, p. 219.

[47] *Ibid*.

[48] Discussed further in the next Chapter.

techniques and especially a sole focus on drugs can, as mentioned, only repress the essential human need for meaning.

Polak wrote that "the spiritual crisis, the crisis of conscience, despair – both of oneself and of a meaning in life – represents the essential domain of existential analysis".[49] At the noetic level, logotherapy comes fully into its own. Here, a different skill of the therapist must come into play, an ability, in Lukas' words, noetically to stimulate the patient. Frankl's virtuosity in this regard was his ability to help the patient to see the redemptive, meaning-laden opportunity awaiting actualization in the moment. In his own words: "I can see beyond the misery of the situation to the potential for discovering a meaning behind it, and thus to turn *an apparently meaningless suffering into a genuine human achievement*."[50]

Here, however, the *objective moral* framework of logotherapy returns. Allport and others[51] had observed that certain espoused values – especially those of extremist and terrorist regimes – even when these took a religious veneer, in fact represent a distorted, a "sick" psyche. Similarly, it is necessary for the therapist to have a sense of the objective values of universal conscience, whereby to help the patient return to the actual seat of conscience, the spiritual itself. The therapist may not confirm a psychopathology as an expression of "conscience"[52].

The same principle applies to interventions at all levels of psychic disturbance. Lukas writes that "out of the practice of psychotherapy, we know many psychic disturbances are nothing more than the not-being-in-harmony with one's conscience, that is, living contrary to one's better self"[53]. She cites instances of values which are at variance with conscience and the therapist must guard against values which represent a pathology rather than a true expression of the spirit.[54] The logotherapist must have a knowledge of the spirit's moral compass.

---

[49] *Ibid.*, p. 13.

[50] *Recollections*, p. 53. "The logotherapist has to do with concrete opportunities of meaning, awaiting the concrete patients sitting before him or her, which can be actualized by them alone" *("Gespräch mit Viktor Frankl", op cit.* p. 23).

[51] See G. Allport, *The Individual and His Religion,* NY: Macmillan, 1960, Theodor W. Adorno *et al., The Authoritarian Personality,* NY: W.W. Norton, 1969.

[52] Lukas, *op. cit.*, p. 63, writes, "In … logotherapy …[w]hen what the patient says contains elements of questionable ethics or is psycho-hygienically questionable, *generating a dysfunction or maintaining a dysfunction* [my emphasis], it is brought before the conscience of the patient . It is placed before a court, as it were, in which the patient is judge and jury, and the therapist ought to act as the occasion arises as advocate and defender for psychic health and human dignity."

[53] *Op. cit.*, p. 23.

[54] *Ibid.*, pp. 23-24, 61-62, citing Frankl.

CHAPTER 2

THE SPIRITUAL CLARIFICATION OF FRANKL'S LOGOTHERAPY

The personality and the soul

In this chapter we follow a number of concepts underlying Frankl's logotherapy to their sources in religious tradition, where they receive further specification and clarification. These are (1) the "soul" (or conscience) understood in relation to the structure of human personality (2) the meaning of the soul's "imitation of G-d" as the fount of ethical personality and (3) the idea of the therapeutic elicitation of meaning and purpose in accordance with the soul or conscience.

Of importance to the concept of the soul in relation to Frankl's psychological model of personality is his attribution of the source of this model to the writings of the great Rabbi Judah Loew, known as the "Maharal" of Prague:

I cite him [the Maharal] in two or three of my books for he was indeed a forerunner of what I term Dimensional Ontology[1].

Neither I, nor a number of Frankl experts, whom I have consulted, have, to the present, been able to locate the places in "two or three of my books" which cite the Maharal as the source (forerunner) of this key doctrine of Frankl. This does not prevent us, however, from going directly to the work of the Maharal himself for the original doctrine[2]. Indeed, the template of Frankl's model of personality shows an extraordinary congruence with, and receives further

---

[1] Viktor E. Frankl and Pinchas Lapide, *G-ttsuche und Sinnfrage*, Gütersloh, Gütersloher Verlagshaus, 2005, p. 58.

[2] See Maharal, *Derech Chayim,* the Maharal's commentary on the Mishnaic Tractate *Pirkei Avos*, (*Ethics of the Fathers)*: specifically Chapter 4:14 (*"shlosha k'sorim heim"*), Chapter 4:22 (*"hakina, v'hataiva v'hakovod")*, Chapter 5:19 (*"talmidov shel Avrohom Ovinu…talmidov shel Bilaam HaRosha")*. See also *"Inyonei arba malchiyos"* in the Maharal's *Ner Mitzvah*; and Chapter 66 of his work *G'vuros HaShem*. These form principal sources for the spiritual clarification of key concepts of Frankl in this chapter.

clarification from, the work of the Maharal.

The Maharal delineates three dimensions or faculties of human personality, which parallel the elements which Frankl identifies, and *the way* Frankl characterises them. There is also in the Maharal's discussion a fourth dimension: the spirit or a fundamental orientation, which pervades and influences all of the three faculties of personality. This fourth dimension in fact helps to clarify a matter which is sometimes blurred in Frankl's work. It is the difference between this "spirit" and *all* of the three faculties of human personality, *including* the highest, the "noetic" or "meaning", faculty. Let us take these in turn, beginning with the first three dimensions and then the fourth.

Just as Frankl distinguishes "bodily" ("somatic"), "mental", and "noetic" (or meaning-supplying) faculties in human personality, so does the Maharal of Prague. The Maharal distinguishes the first of these faculties as primarily "physical" (*gufni*). It has an appetitive and desiring character. It is naturally drawn towards physical gratification and material aggrandizement. Of the three faculties it is the least naurally inclined towards spirituality, for in its raw, uncultivated state it is self-absorbed. This equates, in Frankl's model, to the bodily or somatic dimension of personality.

The second dimension, which the Maharal variously calls vital (*chiyuni*) or self-conscious (*nafshi*), is intelligent (though, in its raw state, this refers to a strategic rather than a moral intelligence). Unlike the first, physical dimension, which experiences unmediated and unreflected desire, it is capable of a "mediating", self-distancing, "judging" and evaluating stance: it grasps the desiring self in relation to others and in regard to considerations outside that self. Whilst the raw physical self merely knows and desires what *it* wants, the (also raw) mental-perceptual self relates, and evaluates itself in relation, to others. So, for example, it is capable of jealousy when it sees *another* who has more than it does. Frankl's name for this perceptual and self-aware self is the *psychological* or mental self.

The third dimension, which the Maharal calls the "intellectual soul" (*nefesh hasichlis*) is different from the foregoing level of "intellect". That lower level of intellect works strategically, "close to the ground". Both the desiring and conscious selves are prone to biases and interests. The "intellectual soul" by comparison is fitted for, and capable of, an abstract concern with a higher meaning. It has to do with the "global" world-views *for which* a person lives, and in the service of which mind and body are directed.

This is the highest faculty of the person in the sense that it can subordinate both the physical and mental dimensions. In ordering them it also *unifies* them. It "tells" the lower – vital, self-conscious – level of intellect how, and with which limitations, it should allow the fulfilment of which physical desires and needs. In this sense, the Maharal called this faculty the "unitive" faculty.

> The parts of the human being are body and mind [here termed *nefesh*]. The human being *as a whole* comprises these parts, in that through them [together], *the person receives the form of the human.* This third dimension is like a house, which has as its parts wood and stones, but afterwards is made a house, compounded of both. It is something other than its parts.[3]

This equates with what Frankl called the noetic (the meaning-finding) faculty inasmuch as it seeks a higher meaning, a "Logos". He stated similarly that this higher self had body and mind "at its disposal" in the service of its purpose.

Whilst this third faculty abstracts away from the prompts and interests of the lower faculties towards a higher meaning, this does not mean that it accomplishes true self-transcendence and that it arrives at the acknowledgment and "imitation" of G-d. It *too* – like physical inclinations and mental perception can be ethically false and biased by interests. Its world-view can be ideological. Frankl acknowledges this when he speaks of the meaning-complexes of cultural ideologies which usurp the noetic faculty and draw it away from true self-transcendence. Frankl gives to these non-self-transcending meanings the title of "collective neuroses" or "pathologies" of the *Zeitgeist* (the "spirit of the times"). Max Weber also spoke of comprehensive "world-views" as expressions of varying "dynamics of interests", which are yet presented as "ideals"[4]. Such world-views are comprehensive justifications of specific interests or biases. The Maharal of Prague speaks of the characteristic corruption of this faculty in the

---

[3] *G'vuros HaShem*, Chapter 66. Translated by S. D. Cowen in "The Maharal of Prague on the Noahide Laws. A translation of *G'vuros HaShem*, Chapter 66", *Journal of Judaism and Civilization*, Vol. 4 (2002), p. 8.

[4] "Interests, material as well as ideal, not ideas directly control action. But world images, which are the product of ideas, have often served as the channels along which action is moved by the dynamics of interests. After all, it is in response to an image of cosmological order whence the question arises from what and towards what one needs to be saved" (Quoted in G. Roth and W. Schluchter, *Max Weber's Vision of History – Ethics and Methods*, Berkeley and Los Angeles: University of California Press, 1979, p. 15). Weber, the personally irreligious sociologist of religion, saw religious world-views as "dynamics of interests". I would seek to turn this around and say (with the Maharal and Frankl) that his description of a world-view, as the expression of a "dynamic of interests", fits essentially *non*-religious, *non*-self-transcending world-views.

qualities of conceit and vainglory (*kovod*) which it experiences in its sensed prowess and "superior" understanding.

The Maharal explains that it is the fourth dimension which determines the character of all the three above-described faculties of the human being, including the highest (for Frankl, the noetic, and for the Maharal, the unitive, faculty). The Maharal approaches the idea of this orienting spirit by exploring a polar antithesis between two biblical personalities, Abraham and the heathen prophet Bilaam. Abraham represented the essence of the spiritual – that is to say, complete emancipation from the sway of physicality In Franklian terms, Abraham was able to achieve complete self-transcendence: no interest in the psychophysical realm could distract him from his attachment to G-d or from fulfilment of the Divine will. Bilaam was the opposite. Gifted with prophetic powers, matching those of Moses, Bilaam was nevertheless wholly immured in the realm of materiality. His animating spirit was the antithesis of self-transcendence: ultimate, consuming self-absorption and self-seeking gratification. The difference in the fundamental orienting "spirit" of these polar opposites played out in the three faculties of their personalities. Bilaam (1) in the bodily realm lusted for gross and unnatural sexual gratification as well as money (2) his mind was distorted by arrogance and (3) his global world-view was wholly geared towards evil and harm. On the other hand, from Abraham's spirit of total self-transcendence followed (1) an abnegation of all unnecessary desire, (2) a humility of thought and (3) a global outlook of goodness and kindness. The same is true for the "students" of Bilaam and Abraham – that is the personalities guided by the same respective "spirits".

In other words, the *human soul in its self-transcendence* was wholly manifest within Abraham and wholly obscured within Bilaam. The nature of the soul *is* self-transcendence. It abnegates all personal interest, because its sole desire is to be drawn to that from whence it comes, namely G-d. It imitates or models the attributes of the Divine and carries out their translation in ethical character and conduct. Whilst the proper principal residence of the soul is the noetic faculty, its will is felt in, and shapes, also the faculties subordinate to the noetic realm: those of intellect and physical feeling. The soul – which actualizes itself as Divine likeness – is a *potential (yecholis)* within the human being: it can be expressed, more or less revealed and dormant, more or less concealed, within the human being. The orientation of self-transcendence is the same as re-awakening and assertion of the soul within the human being[5].

---

[5] See *Likkutei Sichos*, Vol. 15, pp. 58-62, where it is explained that what orients the faculty

Where the soul is repressed, a *contrary* spirit asserts itself within the person, and makes itself manifest within the faculties of human personality.

There are, as noted, in the work of Frankl, occasional confusions between the soul and the noetic faculty. This confusion exists in the identification of the "spirit" with the noetic faculty itself, as against the "psychophysical" faculties. Sometimes the noetic is identified with the spirit or soul *itself*, and sometimes it is identified with the meaning *faculty*. The reality is that the soul has to contend not only with the bodily and mental dimensions, but *first and foremost* with its contenders for dominion within the noetic *faculty*. Frankl, in fact acknowledges this when he speaks, as noted, of *pathologies* which can arise within and usurp the noetic faculty.

Thus, Frankl writes, "No'ogenic neuroses are illness 'from the spirit' – but they are not illness 'in the spirit'. There are no no'oses"[6]. To translate this a little more plainly, pathologies which arise within the (noetic) meaning faculty, are "from" –the noetic faculty which *should* be occupied by – "the spirit". They are "generated" within the noetic faculty (they are no'ogenic). But in the soul which struggles to become the master of the noetic faculty, there is no sickness; there is no neurosis of the soul *(no'osis)*. Confusion arises when both the soul and the faculty, which the soul struggles to occupy and is properly its realm, are both called *no'os*.

Pathologies of the noetic faculty can be the deepest pathologies. A human being, in his or her lower faculties, may appear to "function well", and yet is living according to a pathological world-view which contradicts the human spiritual essence. Whether this is the concentration camp guard, who after a day of unspeakable cruelty, comes home to a "happy home life", or the "high functioning" executive who lives according a deviant sexual ethic, the pathology is real despite the absence of any conscious sense, or outwardly manifest signs, of unwellness. The delusion of "wellness" in the person with a pathological world-view, however, betokens a deeper unwellness. Indeed, the

---

of the "intellectual soul" towards G-d, and activates within it the "Divine likeness" *(tzelem Elokim),* is essentially the beacon of the Divine itself, the tradition – the "great voice" – which comes down from Mt Sinai. The Jewish people from the time of Sinai received the extra dimension of a "G-dly soul" which rivets the intellectual soul towards G-d, though this soul too can be submerged and concealed within a Jew. It is the beacon from Sinai, carried within the Jewish people – a "light to the nations" – that activates the Divine likeness in humanity and orients humanity to imitation of G-d in fulfilment of the Noahide laws, as discussed in the next section.

[6] *On the Theory and Therapy of Mental Disorders*, p. 177.

Maharal indicates that a corrupted noetic pathology will eventually percolate into the subordinate faculties of bodily emotion and mental perception, and corrupt – bringing disorder (and we could add manifestly experienced unwellness) to – these, too.

The concept of the soul redefines the meaning and purpose of human freedom. Without the conscious presence of the soul, the human being is driven by psychophysical interests or cultural ideologies, which, with their "ideals" and "meanings", simply rationalize interests. It is the soul, with its aspiration towards transcendence and transcendent values, which provides the only real alternative to psychophysical and cultural-ideological interests arising in the immanent worldly arena. The "freedom" to choose *between* interests is thus not an ultimate freedom. Authentic freedom is the ability to *transcend* – that is not be driven by – interest itself. In simpler terms, freedom is the ability to choose, as mentioned, between what factual "I" (the faculties of personality with their fortuitous content) want of life and what life (the Creator, with whom the soul, the ultimate "I", is aligned) wants of me.

The soul and ethical personality

Frankl's statement that the "true discovery of the human, the *inventio hominis*, occurs in the *imitatio Dei* [the imitation of G-d]" means that the essential person is an ethical person. The term "ethical", moreover, relates both to the content and structure of personality. How the concept of the "imitation of G-d" supplies both ethical content to, and relates to the structure of personality, is also clarified in the work of the Maharal of Prague.

The meaning of the "imitation of G-d" in the tradition from Sinai is the imitation, to the degree humanly possible, of G-d's attributes. Just as G-d is kind, so should one be kind; just as G-d is just, so should one be just; just as G-d is merciful so should one be merciful and so forth[7]. Of concern to us here are seven Divine attributes and the G-dly behaviours through which a human imitates them in performance of the Seven Noahide laws. We have already made reference in the Preface to these laws, given by G-d to humanity from its beginnings and authoritatively reiterated at Sinai. They are laws relating to forbidden sexual relations, the belief in G-d, the reverence for G-d, prohibitions

---

[7] These attributes do not ultimately inhere within G-d, Who is beyond all description. They were created by Him, through which to build and conduct the Creation. They are also replicated, on a human scale, in the soul, through which the human experiences a fundamental "affinity" and communication with the Divine. See *The Theory and Practice of Universal Ethics – the Noahide Laws*, Chapter 1.

of theft and material harm, the precept of systems of justice, the prohibition of killing and the proper treatment of nature. Starting as a complete code from Noah, the survivor of the biblical flood, they supply the root, core spiritual consciousness of the cultures of his descendants, namely, all humanity.

The Maharal relates these seven universal laws to the structure of human personality itself: (A) to the pervading spirit or soul and (B) to the three faculties of personality, as these in turn each function in the two dimensions of human conduct, namely (1) between the person and G-d and (2) between persons. This is summarized in the following diagram, which we proceed to explain:

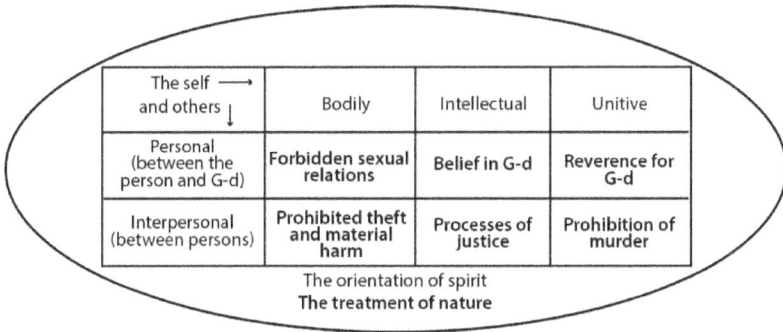

The self → and others ↓	Bodily	Intellectual	Unitive
Personal (between the person and G-d)	Forbidden sexual relations	Belief in G-d	Reverence for G-d
Interpersonal (between persons)	Prohibited theft and material harm	Processes of justice	Prohibition of murder

The orientation of spirit
The treatment of nature

The spirit of self-transcendence

Separate from, though pervading, the basic matrix of human personality (the three faculties in their personal and interpersonal dimensions) is an orienting "spirit". It is this spirit (discussed in the previous section) which either fundamentally disposes the human being towards or against the fulfilment of Divine (– the Noahide –) laws. The Noahide law which itself elicits the self-transcending human soul or spirit and so prepares the human personality for fulfilment of the remaining Noahide laws (and thereby the imitation of the Divine) is a commandment relating to the treatment of nature. So, it also functions to negate the "contrary" spirit, that would orient the person to vitiate fulfilment of the Noahide laws. This is framed biblically as a prohibition on the consumption of the limb of a living animal.

The explanation of this commandment, given by the Maharal, is that even though an animal can be readied for consumption through slaughter, the person who consumes a limb of it whilst it is still alive, at the cost of great suffering to the creature, is not prepared to wait even this little while. Such conduct symbolizes a total and heedless engrossment in the gratification of material and physical desire, which this commandment *negates*. *Positively* expressed, it calls for self-control, in its ultimate form the *transcendence* of personal interest and self-focus. This is the measure of the conscious presence of the soul. Once "activated" through this moral stance, the soul can function in all the other departments of the matrix of personality to produce ethical behaviour[8]. This, the "soul" of ethical behaviour, namely the active spirit of self-transcendence, can now be inspected at work in the structure of human personality to give that structure an ethical form and content, as follows.

The personal dimension (between the person and G-d)

The Maharal indicates how the soul's self-transcendence ethically informs the *bodily*, *mental* and *unitive* ("noetic") faculties in the dimension of conduct between the person and G-d. With regard to the *body*, it is clear that the Noahide law governing *sexual morality* has to do with the permissible and impermissible fulfilment of *bodily* desire. Moreover, sexual morality is in the category of law (not so much between persons as) between the person and G-d. This is because the sexual unions prohibited by Noahide law – adulterous, homosexual, incestual and bestial – remain prohibited even when all the parties to the relationship do, or can be construed to, consent to it[9].

The biblical verse states "Therefore a man shall leave his father and mother and cleave to his wife and they will become one flesh"[10]. The way the human came into existence is through the sexual union of male and female[11]. Once born, he or she now heads towards a new union of male and female and through this produces in the next generation a "one-flesh" offspring of their union, which is the person's continuity into the future. Biological continuity and personal identity merge.

Parents, children and grandchildren represent a single spiritual chain and extended identity. The biblical expression, "man *and* woman He [G-d] created them"[12], signifies that the person has his or her ultimate identity through the union of man and woman, who are each halves of one larger composite unit.

---

[8] This commandment, which schematically is the "last" of the Noahide laws given to all humanity, parallels, as the Maharal points out, the last of the Ten Commandments, namely, the prohibition of covetous desire. Its positive implication, the assertion of self-transcendence and negation of self-absorption, is similarly the spiritual precondition for fulfilment of the others of the Ten Commandments.

[9] Adultery also impacts the marriage of *others*, and for this reason additionally has an interpersonal aspect as we find with the other interpersonal Noahide commandments relating to theft, killing and justice which obviate harm between persons.

[10] Genesis 2:24.

[11] Or, with invitro fertilization, through the fusion of their gametes.

[12] Genesis 5:1.

Their complementary union models the unity of "masculine" (transcendent) and "feminine" (immanent) dimensions of the Divine[13]. It channels and sanctifies sexual impulse towards a union which the makes the human into a "unit" modelling the Divine and an agency serving the Divine purpose.

In the dimension of the relationship between the person and G-d, the *intellectual* or mental faculty of personality is directed towards self-transcendence by the Noahide law prohibiting idolatry. Intellect is an instrument which is suited to critique and distancing analysis. So, it can function to examine the "facts" which are handed to it, and not take them simply at "face value". On the psychological plane, intellect can scrutinize the data of mere feeling or mere predisposition: it "decentres" them and subjects them to critique.

Idolatry – prohibited by the Noahide laws – is a cognitive stance which views a part (a "datum") of creation as "absolute", as the all-grounding foundation of reality. It fetishizes a particular entity, which might range from an object, such as the sun or the moon for their worshippers, or in more times it could make a fetish of "money" and "self-made" success; it may also make a particular emotion, such as "love" absolute. Pre-eminently, it expresses itself nowadays in the world-view of materialism, taking the physical world "as all there is". Idolatry is the surrender of intellect to the claim of a specific datum to ultimate reality.

Frankl puts it this way. In the honest – self-transcending – functioning of intellect, all forms and phenomena within creation are merely "relative": they are all creations of the true Absolute, G-d, and have no subsistent foundation in themselves. The true task of thought is to preserve this perspective and not to make anything which is merely relative – a mere fact or creation dependent on its Creator – absolute. Thus, self-transcending thought is led to a concept of G-d, Creator of all, as the "Absolute" and "the Absolute is there only in order *that the relative remain relativized*"[14]. To make the relative absolute is idolatry.

The way in which intellect – in the "private", personal dimension accordingly – functions to serve and express the human imitation of the Divine, is to comprehend all earthly givens as relative, that is, as subordinate to the Creator of all. In this way intellect comes fully into its ow as truly dispassionate. Dispensing with mere preference and disposition, it is built not on "*I* think" or "*I* feel", but is drawn to a selflessly acknowledged truth bigger than

[13] See S. D. Cowen, *Homosexuality, Marriage and Society*, Redland Bay: Connor Court, 2016, Chapter 3.
[14] "Time and Responsibility", below p. 114. Emphasis added.

"I".[15] It submits for its first principles to G-d.

In the personal dimension, finally, the *unitive* faculty of personality, is brought to self-transcendence through the Noahide prohibition on blasphemy. Self-transcendence leads intellect towards G-d, but the highest, unitive or noetic faculty is already uniquely fitted, capable and constitutionally predisposed to *know* G-d. Its challenge is *hubris* – not to *rebel* against the G-d it can so readily acknowledge. Its ethical imperative is therefore to render honour to G-d, not to itself: not to follow an overweening conceit to "supplant" G-d with an "alternative" ideology or world-view of its making. Whilst the idolater has *mistaken* G-d, the blasphemer at some level knows G-d and yet rebels. Against this narcissistic tendency of the highest human faculty, the Noahide law prohibiting blasphemy comes to enforce the self-transcendence of the meaning faculty itself.

The positive expression of the Noahide prohibition on blasphemy is the reverence for, and devotion to, G-d in the service of G-d. It expresses self-transcendence as the readiness to commit the highest, most "prestigious", "knowing" self of the human being to the sanctification of its Creator, G-d. It ensures that the noetic faculty will remain the home of the soul.

The interpersonal dimension

Just as in the dimension of the relationship of the person with G-d, so also in the *interpersonal* realm, the Maharal relates a further three of the Noahide laws to the rectification of the bodily, mental and unitive faculties of personality. First, the *bodily* or material desire which impacts on relationships with other persons is dealt with in the Noahide law of theft and material harm. Theft is the fulfilment of a desire for *another's* property, which the other has not knowingly agreed to give or exchange. Robbing another's person or property is not as serious as murder, but has yet been compared to murder. For it infringes another's *being*[16] *by negating the other's power of ownership. That is to say, in theft one is indifferent to the integrity of another* in respect of their possessions.

The opposite to this, and implicit in the same Noahide commandment, is *positive* regard for another's property such as in returning lost property or in taking measures to protect other's property from harm. Noahide law sets out a continuum in this area from the prohibition of outright theft, through the

---

[15] See *Likkutei Sichos*, Vol. 2, p. 561.

[16] "One who robs his fellow as much as a *p'ruta* [a small coin], is as though he takes his soul…" (*Hilchos g'zeila v'aveida*, 1:13). See *Likkutei Sichos*, Vol. 32, pp. 112ff.

rectification of harm and damages to another, to positive regard for another's person and property. What ultimately assures that theft and material harm will not occur is *regard for another's* material person and property. It entails ultimately a union of reciprocity with the other. The Noahide law prohibiting theft transforms material desire in the way that the Noahide law governing sexuality transforms bodily desire.

In the interpersonal realm, the faculty of *intellect* is directed towards self-transcendence by the Noahide law of justice. This law has to do with the opposing claims and arguments of persons in conflict of claims with one another or with the State. Justice signifies the objective and impartial evaluation of the claims of others. It guards against intellectual *partiality* in assessing the rights and wrongs of other persons.

This operates in the critical and impartial gathering of evidence, the dispassionate judgment of the evidence and determination of punishment, the degree of responsibility of its perpetrator and the social need for deterrence. It is marked by a thinking which excludes the *irruption* of a particular interest or bias in judgment or would lead to the parties to justice being treated unequally or with partiality. The transcending intellect in the personal sphere bans partiality – fetishization of any datum – in relation to G-d in observance of the Noahide prohibition of idolatry; in the interpersonal sphere the Noahide law of justice excludes partiality in the adjudication and judgment of persons. Justice is not simply a requirement of society, but also of the individual in his or her immediate interpersonal sphere in being fair, dispassionate and responsible in one's potential or actual conflicts with others.

In the realm or interpersonal relationships, the Noahide law prohibiting killing, places the *unitive* faculty of personality under the aegis of self-transcendence. As discussed with regard to the personal dimension, the unitive faculty is the faculty fitted to know G-d. There the Noahide prohibition on blasphemy prevents the unitive faculty from striking against G-d. In the interpersonal realm, the prohibition against killing is related to the same. For the essence of the prohibition on killing is that the soul which enlivens a human being is made in the "image of G-d". Consequently, to strike against human life, which bears the stamp and image of the Divine, is to strike Divine property and agency. Every life – every soul – is on a Divine mission and only its Creator and Owner can decide when that mission ends. Positively put, the intention of this Noahide law is, wherever possible, to protect and save life – whether endangered, fetal or terminally ill – at any stage of its mission on earth. The religious tradition states that "Anyone who preserves one person in the world is considered as having preserved the entire world"[17]. Even where the Noahide law commands to take life, such as in self-defence or defence of another, it is in order to save human life and the society which protects life. The unitive or noetic faculty in the self-transcending personality seeks to hallow, in the personal sphere, the Author of life and, in the interpersonal sphere, that which uniquely bears the Author's stamp, human life.

Logotherapeutic practice and universal ethics

The practice of logotherapy requires, first of all, that the self-transcending self, the soul – or conscience, as the secular patient may wish to call it – be summoned within the human being. The evocation of the spirit involves its self-differentiation, as the essential "I", from the pathologies which take hold of any of the faculties of personality. For when I know *that* and *why* the illness is not "I", and recover the full conscious possession of the healthy, spiritual "I", logotherapy can utilize it as a vital, contributory healing force. Frankl writes:

> It is imperative to distinguish sharply between the somatic, the psychological, and the spiritual. In individual cases a delusional jealousy truly is a psychological reaction to a somatic process; but that a paranoid person who is jealous in this manner – as in a concrete case known to us – would not be carried off by his delusion to carry out a murder, but rather goes and comforts and pampers his wife who has become suddenly ill – this is a spiritual change of attitude that must be fully attributed to the spiritual person, who was sane in this regard[18].

Whilst, as discussed above, not only the "somatic" and "psychological", but also the *diseased noetic self* can be opposed to the true spiritual self, the point is clear. The human spirit, with its meaning- and moral compass, exists somewhere, at some level, as a healthy resource in the midst of, and notwithstanding, an unhealthy personality.

Secondly, logotherapy seeks to apply the self-transcending spirit to "existential analysis", to discover the meanings and values for actualization in individual predicaments. As the widest framework, the Noahide laws provide the ethical grid of universal conscience, as Frankl's "forerunner", the Maharal of Prague, demonstrated. In their detail, they have ethical application to each and every

---

[17] Maimonides, *Mishneh Torah, Hilchos Sanhedrin*, 12:3.

[18] *On the Theory and Therapy of Mental Disorders*, p. 66.

moment of an individual's existence. Frankl himself said something very like this when he spoke of the ideal of an education that would

> spur in young people the process of discovery of ethical purpose. Education should be concerned not simply to transmit knowledge, but also to hone the conscience of the young person: that one be sufficiently attuned as to be able to detect the ethical possibilities and imperatives of individual situations. How much more so, in an epoch in which for many the Ten Commandments seem to have lost their validity, must one be empowered to detect the ten thousand commandments (the thousand-fold application of the Ten Commandments) encoded in the ten thousand situations which confront one[19].

Properly, however, it is not so much the Ten Commandments (which were given to the Jewish people), as Frankl here wrote, but rather the universal Seven Noahide laws (also from the same revelation at Sinai) applied in the multiplicity of personal circumstances, that relate to humanity as a whole. Indeed, there is a major overlap between the Noahide laws and the Ten Commandments.

Frankl clearly distinguished moral education and therapy, the former being didactic whilst, in therapy, the patient must also come by him- or herself to a value or meaning insight, in order to "own" it and for it to be therapeutically efficacious. At the same time, as noted in the last Chapter, he felt that therapy could not be morally neutral or relative. The therapist must therefore be a "living example" and prompter of self-transcendence. Logotherapy should lead the patient *towards* his or her *own* discovery or ratification of the values of conscience.

Logotherapy, thirdly, in order to evoke and assert the self-transcending spirit,[20]

---

[19] "Science of the Soul" (below, p. 142). Frankl wrote similarly in the Preface to a volume of lectures delivered in America, published as *The Will to Meaning, op. cit:* "In an age such as ours, in which traditions are on the wane, psychiatry must see its principal assignment in equipping man with the ability to find meaning. In an age in which the Ten Commandments seem to many people to have lost their unconditional validity, man must learn to listen to the ten thousand commandments implied in the thousand situations of which his life consists. In this respect *I hope the reader will find that logotherapy speaks to the needs of the hour.*" pp. ix-x (emphasis added). Frankl also spoke, as we have noted, of a basic typology of responses to life situations as "creative", "attitudinal" and "experiential". Yet all of these have a moral core. They all imply some kind of ethical response.

[20] This paragraph is largely drawn from my essay "Universal Religion, Viktor Frankl and Gordon Allport", *Journal of Judaism and Civilization*, Vol. 4 (2002).

both in Frankl's and in subsequent logotherapeutic work, has developed an armoury of techniques. One of these techniques, established by Frankl himself, is that of "paradoxical intention". This is a process whereby the patient is prompted through various procedures to "laugh" at his or her psychological foible, and thereby to achieve self-detachment from it. Another method is known as "de-reflection". Though this, the patient removes him or herself from self-absorption and preoccupation, to concern with another or with a higher purpose, whereby the malaise naturally corrects itself. A variety of other therapies, such as cognitive behaviour therapy, may of course be ancillary to logotherapeutic technique. Our concern here, at all events, is not so much with practical methods, as with the goals, of logotherapy.

Whilst Frankl, who, in the writings contained in this volume, was committed to an objective ethics of conscience, did not know to identify these with the content of the Noahide laws, (as distinct from the Ten Commandments) in fact his work shows a deep affinity with the Noahide laws. We can see this in his treatment of disorders of the somatic, psychological and noetic levels of personality in ways analogous to their ethical formation by the Noahide laws, as evidenced in the following examples.

In treating cases of sexual impotence – "reactive sexual neuroses" – relating to a *bodily* emotive incapacity, Frankl wrote:

> People with sexual neuroses pervert and degrade sexuality to a mere means to pleasure, while in reality it is a means of expression, namely the expression of a striving for love; to the extent to which the sexual life is taken out of the totality of the love life, to the extent to which the sexual life is disintegrated and isolated, to that same extent do people lose the immediateness (the "not-being-a-means"-ness)... which is a condition and pre-supposition of normal functioning.[21]

Understanding the ethical purpose of sexuality – that it is not simply about personal physical gratification, but that it serves a loving human bond – here

---

[21] *On the Theory and Therapy of Mental Disorders* p. 128. Note Frankl's remark in "Gespräch mit Wolfram Kurz und Viktor Frankl": "The spiritual *[das Geistige]* is the unique human quality, the specifically human. It shows itself for example in the phenomenon of conscience in contradistinction to mere conditioning. Or, it reveals itself in the phenomenon of love in contradistinction to mere sexuality" p. 21 (present writer's translation). See "Liebe und Sex" in Viktor E. Frankl, *Der Mensch vor der Frage nach dem Sinn eine Auswahl aus dem Gesamtwerk*, Munich: Piper, 1979: "human sexuality is dehumanized when it becomes a mere means to the gratification of desire" p. 94 (present writer's translation).

helped to cure a psychological sexual malaise. More than half-a-century later, with the commitment crises caused by *de facto* relationship culture and the morbidity arising from a culture of "gender-fluidity" and "sexual-reassignment" practices, therapy needs to call on many more aspects of the universal ethics of sexuality. Frankl was stating a minimum when he impressed upon his patients that sexuality was not simply about personal gratification, but has an ethical content. That is the *starting point* of the Noahide law of sexuality, about which there is much more to say.

In a second example – this time of a mental-perceptual (as distinct from bodily) personality disorder – Frankl speaks of a nurse who had fallen into depression because, as a result of illness, she was no longer able to work. He relates:

> As soon as you start to despair over your situation, I told her, it is as if the meaning of human life stands or falls with whether a person is able to work so and so many hours; but with this you deny all the ill and the infirm every right to life and every justification for their existence...[W]hereas until now you were never able to do more for all those people entrusted to you than provide them your professional assistance, now you have the chance to be more, namely, to be a human example.
>
> These few suggestive words must suffice to show that even in cases of completely understandable – indeed seemingly justified – despair, it is possible to turn a depression around. One only has to know that all despair is ultimately one thing: idolatry – the absolutization of a single value (in the above case the idolization of the value of being able to work)[22].

Frankl made this patient aware that fixation on (making "absolute") a single (thwarted) value, symptomized here in depression, was *unethical*. Frankl profoundly observed that this is a subtle kind of "idolatry" (and indeed applies in concept to the Noahide law prohibiting idolatry). This understanding, on the part of the patient, which is resonant with objective conscience, gave her the power of conscience in her therapeutic struggle with depression.

Thirdly, with regard to the unitive, noetic dimension, we find the example of the therapy, which Frankl practised on himself, in regard to the suicidal ideation which visited him in the concentration camp, as narrated in the last chapter. It led him to see that an ideation – a "reason" – to end his life, was by

---

[22] *On the Theory and Therapy of Mental Disorders,* p. 218.

definition a false ideation or reason. Life is above all a *summons* to *live* ethical meaning. This chimes with the Noahide law prohibiting murder (and suicide) since the human being is the bearer of a soul with a Divine imprint and on a Divine *mission* and as such is inviolable. Suicide is ultimately unethical.

In each of these three cases, it was an ethical principle consonant with the Noahide laws that was adduced to cure a corruption – with attendant experienced malaise – of feeling, of perception and of supposed purpose and meaning. Frankl's logotherapy is a refined prototype of a psychology of the *moral structure of personality* based on the universal ethical content of conscience or soul, the Noahide laws.

CHAPTER 3

FRANKL AND THE
RECLAMATION OF FREUD

Frankl and the reclamation of Freudian theory

The path leading to the creation of Frankl's logotherapy began, as we saw in Chapter 1, with a *rejection* of Freud. Frankl categorically rejected Freud's reduction of the human personality to an instinctual structure which *wholly drove* ("pan-deterministically") the human being to certain behaviours. Logotherapy made this good by restoring human choice, based on the ability of a person to draw upon the human spirit's power of defiance of mere instinct and "conditioning". At the same time, whilst logotherapy opened to the human *spirit* and sought to restore its sovereignty throughout the human, Frankl was clearly aware that logotherapy was not a science of the *psychophysical* dimensions of personality. To work with the "psychophysical organism", that is to say, with body and mind, *their* science – psychotherapy – was also needed.

Here, fascinatingly, Frankl called upon the psychoanalysis of Freud – the ostensible great antagonist of the spirit and the foundations of logotherapy – as a primary exemplar of a psychotherapy which could work with logotherapy. In one passage, Frankl speaks of Freud in the same breath as he speaks of the spiritual ancestor of his logotherapy, the Maharal of Prague:

> When we visit the oldest used synagogue in the world, the Alt-Neu-Schule in Prague, the guide shows us two seats – on one sat the famous, legendary Rabbi Loew (of whom it is said that he created Golem out of a lump of clay) and on the other sat all the other rabbis since; for none dared to set himself equal to Rabbi Loew and take his seat. And so it is that through the centuries the seat of Rabbi Loew remains unclaimed. I believe

it is the same with Freud: no one will ever be able to measure up to him[1].

With this acknowledgment by Frankl of Freud, one wonders how Freud can be drawn into synthesis with Frankl's own work, when the frameworks of their theories of human personality clash so fundamentally. Frankl suggests an answer in a footnote to another piece:

Existential analysis [logotherapy's therapeutic instrument] is no substitute for the psychotherapy which has been developed up until now. Rather it constitutes its necessary supplementation. In many ways the discoveries of Freud retain their validity. Thus, for example, the theory of dreams will continue to maintain its validity. However, it is not [the essential, spiritual] "I", who dreams, but rather the "Id" [the somatic level of personality, which] dreams in me, and within the dynamics of the "Id", psychoanalytic theory continues to have its validity[2].

Similarly, when Frankl writes with regard to Freudian psychoanalysis,

It is certainly true that the Id drives, but it is thereby forgotten, that the "I" wants, that the "I" – decides![3]

he is stating that we *can learn* from Freud about the content of the Id, the somatic dimension, but psychoanalysis must yet be integrated with logotherapy, which maintains the free choosing role of the spiritual "I". In other words, there is a therapeutic "science" of the soul and its evocation within the person – logotherapy – *and* a science of the psychophysical organism or the bodily and mental dimensions of personality – psychotherapy. Frankl was open to the use of a variety of psychotherapies (not only Freud's) in conjunction with logotherapy. Each psychotherapy could operate with its methods, germane to the psychophysical self, to bring that self into alignment with the spiritual consciousness (and "demands") of the human being.

What interests us here is what, for Frankl, might be construed as the unrivaled power and potential in Freudian psychoanlaysis ("no one will ever be able to measure up to him"). In the remainder of this chapter, we explore both the paradox and explanation of Frankl's implicit ideal of a reclamation of Freudian psychotherapy for use in "synthesis" with his logotherapy. This involves us in

---

[1] *On the Theory and Therapy of Mental Disorders*, p. 239.

[2] *"Die Existenzanalyse und die Probleme der Zeit"*, in Frankl, *Logos und Existenz*, Vienna: Amandus Verlag, 1951, pp. 38-39. Present writer's translation.

[3] *Ibid.*, p. 38.

examining (1) the Freudian "pantheon" of pristine human instincts in the remainder of this section, (2) in the second section of this chapter, Frankl's relation to the Freudian instincts in their "pristineness" and the requirement of their reorientation and transformation and (3) in the third section, the idea of a developmental dynamic of that reorientation and transformation of instincts under the aegis of Frankl's key concept of "responsibility".

Freud dignified the raw or pristine instincts powering human personality with the names of Greek deities and mythic figures – amongst which we here discuss *Eros*, *Thanatos*, and *Narcissus*. With these personifications, he gave expression to the full pagan potencies of the instincts within the person – willful masters unto themselves. These three instinctual complexes are linked with, or primarily located in, different faculties of personality: the physical, mental and "Superego", or what Frankl would call noetic consciousness. They constitute often early, but at all events untamed, states of these faculties.

The primary instinct of the bodily dimension of personality in Freudian theory is *Eros* – libido with its questing of sexual gratification and release. Of this instinct there is substantial discussion in Freud's writings. The bodily faculty of personality is called by Freud the "Id", literally the "It", and Eros is the primary instinct which occupies it.

In Freudian theory, the second, mental faculty of personality is termed the "Ego". The major instinct which inhabits it is called *Thanatos*, the death – sometimes also called the aggressive or destructive – instinct. Of this instinct there is much less, in fact only fragmentary, discussion in Freud's writings. In *Beyond the Pleasure Principle*, Freud writes:

> [W]e must admit the critics to be in the right who from the first have suspected that psycho-analysis makes sexuality the explanation of everything…This result was at all events one not intended by us. On the contrary, we took as our starting point a sharp distinction between the ego-instincts (= death-instincts) and the sexual instincts (= life-instincts). We were prepared indeed to reckon even the alleged self-preservative instincts of the ego among death-instincts, a position which we have since corrected and withdrawn from. Our standpoint was a dualistic one from the beginning, and is so to-day more sharply than before, since we no longer call the contrasting tendencies egoistic and sexual instincts, but life-instincts and death-instincts[4].

---

[4] *The International Psycho-analytical Library*, Ed. Ernest Jones No. 4S. Freud, *Beyond the*

In *Civilization and Its Discontents*, Freud writes similarly:

> Starting [in *Beyond the Pleasure Principle*] from speculations on
> the beginning of life and from biological parallels, I drew the
> conclusion that, besides the instinct to preserve living substance
> and to join it into ever larger units [i.e. Eros], there must exist
> another, contrary instinct seeking to dissolve those units and to
> bring them back to the primaeval, inorganic state. That is to say,
> as well as Eros there was an instinct of death.[5]

Freud would elaborate this instinct as one which controls, limits and restrains the expression of Eros, the sexual instinct. Residing within the mental, as distinct from the physical dimension of personality, it operates to review and control physical impulse in accordance with the "Reality Principle".

Freud then spoke of a third element, to which he did not affix the term "instinct", but which we might say has the quality of an instinct. It inhabits the third faculty of personality, known as the "Superego". This instinct, or driving force, is named for the mythic Narcissus, the son of a Greek god Cephissus, who one day caught sight of his own reflection in a stream and became enchanted with it – that is, with himself. Freud associated this with a *self*-love, which, heightened, results in something like "megalomania", the very opposite of one who loves *another*; for, as Freud states, "a person in love [i.e., with another] is humble."[6]

In Freudian theory, the Id (the object-focused, desiring self) and the Ego (the managing, perceptual[7], self-reviewing self) in their pristine relationship

Pleasure Principle, translated by C.J.M. Hubback, London and Vienna: The International Psychoanalytical Press, 1922, p. 43 (Rosings digital publications).

[5] *Civilization and its Discontents*, (transl. J. Riviere, revised and edited by J. Strachey, London: Hogarth Press and the Institute of Psycho-Analysis, 1963), p. 55. Freud also summarized somewhat tentatively these two instincts in the following terms: "The upshot of our enquiry so far has been the drawing of a sharp distinction between the 'ego-instincts' and the sexual instincts, and the view that the former exercise pressure towards death and the latter towards a prolongation of life. But this conclusion is bound to be unsatisfactory in many respects even to ourselves" Sigmund Freud, *Beyond the Pleasure Principle* (transl. J. Strachey), N.Y.: Dover, 2015, p. 37.

[6] Sigmund Freud, "On Narcissism" (1914) in J. Strachey ed., The Standard Edition of the Complete Psychological Works of Sigmund Freud, Volume XIV (1914-1916): *On the History of the Psycho-Analytic Movement, Papers on Metapsychology and Other Works*, 1948 Printing, p. 98.

[7] "...perceptions may be said to have the same significance for the ego as instincts have for the id." Sigmund Freud, *The Ego and the Id*, transl. Joan Riviere, revised and edited

work together: the Ego is the strategic procurer and warden of the desires of the Id. When, however, the Id is for some reason unable to achieve its objects, and the failure is either accepted or forced by the Ego, a new dimension arises within personality. The Id transfers its "love" from the objects, from which it has been denied gratification, to the very Ego, which has denied them. Object-desiring *Eros* (libido), then becomes a love *for* Ego (ego-libido). Freud writes:

> ...it may be said that this transformation of an erotic object-choice into an alteration of the ego is also a method by which the ego can obtain control over the id and deepen its relations with it – at the cost, it is true, of acquiescing to a large extent in the id's experiences. When the ego assumes the features of the object, it is forcing itself, so to speak, upon the id, as a love-object and is trying to make good the id's loss by saying: 'Look, you can love me too – I am so like the object'.
>
> The transformation of object-libido into narcissistic libido which thus takes place obviously implies an abandonment of sexual aims, a desexualization – a kind of sublimation, therefore[8].

This is the birth of what Freud calls with bitter irony "morality", namely the transfiguration of self-frustration into a loved "ideal". As a forced synthesis of the "id" and "ego" instincts, a "super" self is born, which preens itself on its power to decree its new rules (which Freud calls with the same bitter irony "conscience"). The pristine state of the Superego in the infant is "primary narcissism":

> The charm of a child lies to a great extent in his narcissism, his self-contentment and inaccessibility, just as the charm of certain animals which seem not to concern themselves about us, such as cats and the large beasts of prey. Indeed, even great criminals and humorists, as they are represented in literature, compel our interest by the narcissistic consistency with which they manage to keep away from their ego anything that would diminish it[9].

Indeed, Freud writes that parents often recapitulate their own primary, childhood narcissism "which they have long since abandoned" in their attitude and affection towards their baby:

> The child shall have a better time than his parents; he shall not

---

by James Strachey, London: The Hogarth Press, 1962, p. 20.

[8] *Ibid.*, p. 20.

[9] *Ibid.*, p. 89.

be subject to the necessities which they have recognized as para-
mount in life. Illness, death, renunciation of enjoyment, restric-
tions on his own will, shall not touch him; the laws of nature
and of society shall be abrogated in his favour; he shall once
more really be the centre and core of creation – 'His Majesty the
Baby', as we once fancied ourselves[10].

Freud identifies and affirms this trio of pristine instincts, personified as
Eros, Narcissus and Thanatos, when he laments the sacrifice to "civilization"
of "[uninhibited] sexual life…the sense of omnipotence […and] the aggressive
or vindictive inclinations in…personality"[11].

Frankl's relation to the Freudian instincts

Freud saw the repression of pristine instincts by what he termed "civilized
morality" as a source of psychological sickness, neurosis. He saw conscience or
spirit itself as a repressive social construct, an internalized "Superego" thwarting gratification of the instinctual life of the human being. For Freud, religion
constituted the preponderant source of this alien and imposed Superego, and
as such was the source of culture's "discontents". Frankl took an opposite view
of religion:

When Freud states, 'Religion is the collective human obsessive
neurosis – similar to the neurosis of the child which arises
from the Oedipus complex, from its relationship to its father
– so are we…close to turning it around and instead wagering
this statement: 'The collective neurosis is the psychological
impairment of the capacity for religiosity"[12].

Frankl reverses the relationship, posited by Freud, between religious spirituality and mental health:

Where the *spiritual* "I" merges into its unconscious depths, that
is, into its foundation, there we speak of conscience, of love,
or of art. Where, to the contrary the *psychophysical* "I" irrupts
into consciousness, there we speak of neurosis or of psychosis
– depending on its pathology, i.e. whether it is psychologically

---

[10] *Ibid.*, p. 91.

[11] "'Civilized' Sexual Morality and Modern Nervous Illnesses" in *Civilization, Society
and Religion*, transl. Angela Richards, Ed. Albert Dickson, The Penguin Freud Library,
Vol. 12, London: Penguin, 1991, p. 38.

[12] *Der Unbewusste G-tt*, Vienna: Amandus Verlag, 1949, p. 106. Present author's translation.

caused (as with neurosis) or somatically caused (as with psychosis).[13]

The template of values known to the spirit, when implemented by the spirit in the lower faculties of personality, refines – and by definition makes healthy – those faculties. On the other hand, the irruption of the untutored, rawly instinctual lower faculties into, and their takeover of, the highest supervising consciousness in the person, has the opposite effect. Wayward impulse and distorted perception receive the "official" sanction of this consciousness and are incubated into full-blown psychosis and neurosis[14].

Frankl did not deny the Freudian depiction and analysis of the pristine instinctual structure (certainly of the psychophysical levels) of personality for the purposes of psychotherapy. Its utility, however, was to be found in

---

[13] *Ibid.*, p. 50. Present author's translation.

[14] Animals are ruled by instinct, without any higher morally arbitrating consciousness, and yet, in their natural habitat, seem generally not prone to "psychosis" and "neurosis". The explanation of this by religious tradition is that animals do not have free choice in relation to the regulation of their instincts; these are regulated for them. Their behaviour and instincts are ruled by a natural order, decreed by G-d, which allows them to function *generally* without the deviations or aberrations, which humans experience as psychological sickness. The human being, on the other hand, who since the sin of the Tree of Knowledge became "like G-d knowing good and evil" (Genesis 3:5) can choose good or evil. That is to say, he or she can heighten or distort impulse and perception into forms which are non-normative and dysfunctional by the standard of conscience. Freud himself intimated this when he spoke of the "polymorphous perverse" attitude, which actually corrupts – or in Freud's word "seduces" – the instincts. Thus, Freud sets out in his second Contribution to the Theory of Sex, "Infantile sexuality": *"Polymorphous-Perverse Disposition.* It is instructive to know that under the influence of seduction, the child may become polymorphous-perverse and may be misled into all sorts of transgressions. This goes to show that the child carries along the adaptation for them in his disposition. The formation of such perversions meets but slight resistance because the psychic dams against sexual transgressions, such as shame, loathing and morality – which depend on the age of the child – are not yet erected or are only in the process of formation. In this respect, the child perhaps does not behave differently from the average uncultured woman in whom the same polymorphous-perverse disposition exists. Such a woman may remain sexually normal under usual conditions, but under the guidance of a clever seducer, she will find pleasure in every perversion and will retain it as her sexual activity. The same polymorphous or infantile disposition fits the prostitute for her professional activity, still it is absolutely impossible not to recognize in the uniform disposition to all perversions, as shown by an enormous number of prostitutes and by many women who do not necessarily follow this calling, a universal and primitive tendency." Sigmund Freud, "Infantile Sexuality" in "Three Contributions to the Theory of Sex" in A. A. Brill (editor and translator), *The Basic Writings of Sigmund Freud*, NY: The Modern Library (Random House), 1938, pp. 592-93.

the treatment of instincts, not in the advocacy for their free release. To the contrary, the methods of psychoanalysis had to be consciously integrated with logotherapeutic principles and its affirmation of human freedom and responsibility:

> …the therapeutic outcome *[Effekt]* in general in psychotherapy
> – indeed in psychiatry – by no means proves the correctness of
> its theoretical assumptions. No doubt, psychoanalysis is effec-
> tive, probably for the reason, that it ultimately *does* contain a
> tacit appeal to the free and responsible "I", which it [in fact]
> presupposes[15].

In other words, Freud may correctly have identified the instinctual structure of personality, and this is of psychotherapeutic importance. The question for Frankl is how to *relate* to the instincts depicted in Freudian psychoanalysis. Let us see now, how Frankl relates to each of the Freudian instincts in terms of the need, not for their release, but rather for their modification.

For Freud, Eros is viewed as essentially the drive for *gratification* of the libidi-nal wishes of the somatic self into the blissful state endorsed by the "Nirvana" principle. It is the instinctual drive towards a state of tensionless gratification that for Freud represents the primary and essentially legitimate "personhood" of the human. His lament is that sexuality has been channeled instead by civilization into reproductive functions in the framework of the family instead of being a value for itself. Accordingly, for Freud, the demands made on Eros by "civilized" conscience and morality convert the human being into a neurotic. Thus, he argues, where greater sexual license is given (as, Freud claims, was given to men in Viennese society) there is better mental health; and where "civilized" sexual morality was imposed (as, Freud claims, was imposed upon women in Viennese society) there is worse, mental health:

> …in many families the men are healthy, but from a social point
> of view immoral to an undesirable degree, while the women are
> high-minded and over-refined, but severely neurotic.[16]

Here, we find a direct clash between Frankl and Freud. Freud maintains that the truly "moral" norm and condition for psychic health is the largely unrestricted gratification of erotic *object*-libido; that is to say, sexual *self*-grat-ification. Frankl, on the other hand, was at pains to elaborate that sexuality, divorced from love for *the other* person is a source of psychological illnesses.

---

[15] *"Die Existenzanalyse und die Probleme der Zeit"*, pp. 38-39. Present author's translation.

[16] "'Civilized' Sexual Morality and Modern Nervous Illness", pp. 43-44.

The example discussed in Chapter 2 is that of sexual impotence. It is only when human sexuality is associated with other-directedness, that is to say, has the moral quality of love, that it can be fully healthy psychologically.

Just as Freud sought the disinhibition of the Id-instinct, libido, and saw in in its moral inhibition the source of neurosis, so too with the Ego-instinct. Here, he referred to the inhibition of aggression (Thanatos) as a victimization of instinct by civilization and a hazard to mental health:

> A similar failure to obtain compensation is to be seen after the suppression of impulses inimical to civilization which are not directly sexual. If a man, for example, has become over-kind as result of a violent suppression of a constitutional inclination to harshness and cruelty, he often loses so much energy in doing this that he fails to carry out all that his compensatory impulses require and he may, after all, do less good on the whole than he would have done without the suppression[17].

We have noted that in Freudian theory the Ego confronts the "Pleasure Principle" of the desiring Id with its own "Reality Principle". That is to say, the "Ego Instinct", as guardian of the Id, surveying the pitfalls and prospects for its instinctual gratification, functions as something of a judge. Its judgment has powers of "punishment", "aggression" and even "vindictiveness", necessary for the task. These too, according to Freud, require unfettered self-expression *elsewhere*.

This function of the Ego, in its raw instinctual form as Thanatos, is, however, susceptible to a two-fold corruption. One is in the *quality* of its judgment and the second is in the *function* of its judgment. As regards the first, the Thanatos or aggression, which Freud would like to disinhibit, all to readily descends into murderous brutality. It is inconceivable that Frankl would regard aggression as a healthy actualization of the Ego-instinct. To the contrary, he witnessed and experienced at first hand possibly the most brutal expression of the aggressive instincts in human history: the Nazi camps of cruelty and annihilation. The true function of the mental faculty (Ego) as judgment – as a norm of conscience and civilization – is one which displays *justice*: balanced and dispassionate assessment. Aggression (partiality and cruelty) is the corruption of judgment.

Secondly, the function of the Ego, in Freud's theory, is to organize a path for the Id, as the *trustee* or *regent* of the Id, in judicious selection or modification of the Id's objects to be attained with its own "Reality Principle". Yet,

---

[17] *Ibid.*, pp. 54-55.

as Frankl writes (as noted in Chapter 1) that the directions for Ego in Freud tend to be a secondary derivation form the primary erotic instincts of the Id inasmuch as Ego tends often to do the Id's bidding rather than to constrains it. Freud says as much in the following vivid analogy of the horse (the Id) and the rider (the Ego):

> The functional importance of the ego is manifested in the fact that normally control over the approaches to motility devolves upon it. Thus, in its relation to the id it is like a man on horseback, who has to hold in check the superior strength of the horse; with this difference, that the rider tries to do so with his own strength while the ego uses borrowed forces. The analogy may be carried a little further. Often the rider, if he is not to be parted from his horse, is obliged to guide it where it wants to go; so in the same way the ego is in the habit of transforming the id's will into action as if it were its own.[18]

The Freudian Ego intelligently takes the Id "where it wants to go" or in other words of Freud, the Ego "is first and foremost a body-ego"[19].

Whilst Freud accords a certain sovereignty to the horse (emotive desire) over its rider (mind), Frankl and the religious tradition insist on the sovereignty of the rider over the horse. Freud's notion that the rider must take the horse where it wants to go for fear of "being separated from the horse" is simply not the recipe of civilization. Most riders master their horses, and it is the quality of intellect, that it is innately endowed with an ability to master emotion. Indeed, Freud acknowledges that "civilization" (ruefully enclosed in quotation marks) has done a very good job at mastering emotion, and could only have done so with the service of the Ego. It is not that intellect *cannot* constrain impulse, but rather that, in his view, it *should not* do so. It seems that, according to Freud, the ego instincts should find release as aggression, but not against the erotic interests of the Id. This is certainly contrary to the role attributed by Frankl (and religious tradition) to the reflective, analytic instrument of reason. Frankl believed that intellect had crucial leverage over emotion, which should be used to draw emotion into alignment with the instructions of conscience.

The "instinct" (though, as noted, he may not have termed it as such) which Freud associates with the faculty that emerges as the Superego, as mentioned, is narcissism. Born out of the failure of the Ego to achieve the Id's erotic wishes,

---

[18] *The Ego and the Id*, p. 15.

[19] *Ibid.*, p. 17

it transfers the Id's libido to the Ego itself, becoming Ego-libido, or self-love. This narcissism transforms the Ego's failure into "altruistic surrender"[20] – surrender to what Freud regards, bitterly, as conscience with its "repressive" religious morality. Already in the infant, this Superego-conscience

> answers to everything that is expected of the higher nature
> of man...it contains the germ from which all religions have
> evolved. The self-judgment which declares that the ego falls short
> of its ideal produces the religious sense of humility to which the
> believer appeals in his longing. As a child grows up, the role of
> the father is carried on by teachers and others in authority; their
> injunctions and prohibitions remain powerful in the ego-ideal
> and continue, in the form of conscience, to exercise the moral
> censorship. The tension between the demands of conscience
> and the actual performances of the ego is experienced as a sense
> of guilt. Social feelings rest on identifications with other people,
> on the basis of having the same ego-ideal.[21]

Freud rejected the "humility" associated with conscience and religion as the mere façade of a Superego, which wrought repression of the instinctual self. The instinct, which he wished to release in its place, was a narcissism ("the sense of omnipotence") which, garbed in a cultural ideology inspired by Freud, overturned the morality transmitted by religion. For Frankl, on the other hand, humility was no deceit. It was the hallmark of human self-transcendence, the stimulant of the soul or conscience, through which the "*true* discovery of the human ... occurs in the imitation of G-d."

The developing mastery of instinct

We have quoted Frankl's conditions for the validity and application of Freudian psychoanalysis in conjunction with logotherapy. These are found (1) not in Freud's "theoretical assumptions" that the human being is exclusively instinctually driven – but in the logotherapeutic acknowledgment that there

---

[20] See Anna Freud, *The Ego and the Mechanisms of Defence*, Revised Ed'n, London: the Hogarth Press and the Institute of Psycho-Analysis, 1968, p. 134.

[21] *The Ego and the Id*, p. 27. Anna Freud in *The Ego and the Mechanisms of Defence*, p. 7, writes: "In the id the...sovereign principle which governs the psychic processes is that of obtaining pleasure. In the ego, on the contrary, the association of ideas is subject to strict conditions, to which we apply the comprehensive term 'secondary process'; further, the instinctual impulses can no longer seek direct gratification – they are required to respect the demands of reality and, more than that, to conform to ethical and moral laws by which the superego seeks to control the behavior of the ego."

is also a spiritually deciding "I"; (2) that Freud has correctly perceived the instinctual makeup of personality – but that this is the makeup of the "raw" personality; and (3) that psychoanalysis must explicitly admit the role of spiritually-informed deciding "I" into dynamic, developmental engagement with instinct.

This means further that application of Freudian insights and methods require surrender of any concept of the "virtue" of the pristine instincts of infancy. That is a time when the spiritually conscious "I" is not yet a power to deal with them. It entails acknowledgment that the "repression" or sublimation of instincts, as maturation proceeds, has a vital and positive aspect. Finally, it involves the recognition that the ideal actualization of instincts consists not their simple gratification, but in their refinement or transformation.

The concept of responsibility, at the foundation of Frankl's logotherapy, implies – beyond the arousal of self-transcendence and hence the spiritual, within the person – that the psychophysical self *be aligned* with the spirit's template of meaning and ethical value. Logotherapy sets the goal, but as Frankl pointed out, it calls on psychotherapy for help with the means. To accomplish a synthesis of logotherapy with the Freudian theory of the instincts, the latter needs to be reworked and reemployed in terms of a developmental dynamic of responsibility[22]. This involves the progressive control and transformation of the instincts, passing through three stages – "pre-responsibility", "basic responsibility" and "complete or automatic responsibility" – as indicated and elaborated by the religious tradition from Sinai, to which Frankl paid respect[23].

The first stage is the *pre-responsible* stage of childhood. A child is born with an unruly emotional complex in full force. Childhood is a stage at which intellect – in its regulative power equipped for the control of emotion – is not yet developed. The child thus does not possess the ability to discriminate amongst and check impulses: it is ruled by them. The child is angered by a small

---

[22] Frankl used the term "responsibility" in terms of readiness and ability to "answer" to life's predicaments in a meaningful way; as he put it, "response-ability." We here combine with the readiness to respond, the how to respond: the individual's answering to conscience as this is formed in the ethical "imitation of G-d", also vital to Frankl's thought. "Responsibility" thereby signifies the ability to answer with one's psychophysical being to the demands of conscience.

[23] Much of the following draws, sometimes *verbatim*, on S. D. Cowen, "The concept of a person: reflections on Judaism and psychotherapy", *Journal of Judaism and Civilization*, Vol. 1 (1998), pp.32-37.

thing: emotion is *disproportionate* to the value or importance of its object[24]. Emotion in childhood is in varying degrees unbridled. So too, childishness in an *adult* is the eclipse of the quality of intellectual review and its defeat before insurgent emotion.

Intellect, as a regulator of emotion, is, however, in a process of development within the child towards "responsibility" defined as an ability to check emotion in accordance with norms of conduct. The attainment of a basic level of responsibility – such as that associated with legal liability and certain forms of contract – occurs, in the tradition from Sinai, in early adolescence. Prior to that point the person is not legally liable for his or her acts. Inasmuch as the intellectual regulatory power in a child is in the process of growth, there is a certain "superiority" of the child over the adult mentally infirm person in that the child "will *come* to a stage of responsibility"[25]. Consequently, there is an obligation to educate the child in ethical commandments inasmuch as this knowledge is necessitated by his or her instantaneous moral obligation and liability, on reaching this first stage of "majority"[26].

This second stage of moral personality development we call in a legal sense, without further qualification, "basic responsibility". Even where a child may comprehend, conceptually and analytically, and accept norms of conduct, it lacks the quality of responsibility, signified by the ability to translate the understanding and acceptance of these norms into *stably and consistently* regulated action[27]. At the age of legal responsibility for action, the development of the intellect pertinent to the *stable regulation* of emotion is complete[28]. In the tradition from Sinai, this level is reached by a male at the age of 13 and by a female at the age of 12. It signifies the ability to check and restrain impulse, which left to itself, would lead to the transgression of norms. In Freudian parlance, without the pejorative connotations, it would be called the stable repression or sublimation of impulse. The intellect – informed by conscience – can now assert itself over the appetitive desires of the person. This should not, however, imply a thwarting of *identity* – that intellect represses impulse, producing what Freud would consider "neurosis". For since the person *knows*

---

[24] A young child might throw a tantrum for hours over a candy, an older child will be upset less, and an adolescent might pass over it virtually immediately.

[25] Babylonian Talmud Tractate *Shabbos* 153a Rashi s.v. *l'shoteh*.

[26] See *Likkutei Sichos*, Vol. 17, p. 70 and Vol. 26, p. 75.

[27] See Rabbi Schneur Zalman of Liadi, *Tanya*.

[28] In Jewish law termed *"bar mitzvah"*: 13 for a boy and 12 for a girl.

that it is the will of G-d, and hence one's own spiritual will, to struggle with, and tame one's emotional being, there is no "self-betrayal". Pain, suffering and unease is not a conflict with personal identity, when these are grasped as providential (and meaningful) challenges in the actualization of normative purpose – illuminated and validated by the soul or conscience – in one's life.

Whilst the foregoing stage of basic responsibility achieves the *subordination* of emotions to intellect, there is yet a higher stage of responsibility (in Frankl's sense of answerability to conscience). This third stage occurs when the unique power or force of the emotions in their "own right" and with their full potency are – not simply tamed and restrained but – *transformed and given over* to the purposes which the spirit has for the human being. This is the greatest actualization of emotion. For, it is explained, intellect itself is essentially "cold"; *in itself* it is not strongly impelled to act. Emotions, on the other hand, are *motors or motivators of action*. Religious tradition explains:

> Intellect and excitement are two separate worlds. Intellect – a world cold and settled; excitement – a world seething and impetuous. The human's spiritually mandated service is to combine them, unite them. The impetuousness then becomes transformed into a longing, and the intellect into the guide in a life of service and action[29].

For emotion to become an *equal* (as distinct from subordinate) partner of intellect, it is insufficient for emotion simply to obey – to be constrained or forced – by intellect. It requires also an independent refinement which allows its potency to be brought to the fulfilment of spiritual ideals or norms, without being dampened or subdued by intellect. Such refined emotions thus come to stand, not subordinate to but, *on the level of* intellect[30], because they have their own relationship to the soul without the mediation of intellect. This third level of "complete" or "automatic" responsibility, the purification and true "freeing" of emotion, however, comes after the second level of basic responsibility, where emotion was subjected to the discipline and mediation of intellect. The human being is then ethical (also) *because of* his or her refined emotional qualities. In terms of Freud's metaphor of the horse and rider – far from the rider being led by the horse or even, with a struggle, the rider taking control of the horse – *the horse by itself goes where the rider knows to go*. The age at which a person reaches

---

[29] Rabbi M. M. Schneerson, *Hayom Yom*, English translation by Y.M. Kagan (Kehos: N.Y., 5748) Entry of 12 Sh'vat.

[30] *Likkutei Sichos*, Vol. 39, p. 29, fn. 68

the *potentiality* for this kind of *transformation* (beyond the simple control) of emotion is given in the tradition from Sinai[31] as 20.[32]

How psychotherapy, and particularly a re-oriented Freudian psychoanalysis, might specifically work in with the developmental ascent through the levels of responsibility is not our concern here. One thing, however, does appear from Freud's encounter with a great Rabbi, recounted in the next chapter. Freud, in the moment of that encounter, was able to come beyond the "basement" of human personality to a vision of the culminating development of personality in the transformation of instinct.

---

[31] Rabbi Sholom Dov Ber, *Sefer Maamarim* of the year 5663 (N.Y: Kehos) p. 21. The *halachic* (Jewish legal) expression of this level of development reached at the age of 20 is that is the age at which one comes to liable for punishments meted out at the hands of Heaven, as distinct from those of an earthly court, which apply already to a male of 13, or female of 12, years and one day. So too, the sale made by individuals of these ages is halachically considered a sale. When, however, it comes to selling land (the most serious of possessions) which, moreover, one has simply *inherited* as distinct from having *worked* for, it (and so less easily sensing its value) only the sale of a 20 year old is considered a sale. For then one is presumed to have reached the degree of completeness or fullness of judgment that he or she would not lightly dispose of this in order to obtain cash. See Maimonides, *Hilchos Mechira* 26:13 (based on the Babylonian Talmud, Tractate *Bava Basra* 155a) according to the explanation of the *Gra, Chosheh Mishpot* 235: *s'if koton* 26. This level of development is called, in Chassidic thought, the accomplishment of *mochin d'gadlus* or *mochin b'etzem.*

[32] Denoted in mystical tradition by the Hebrew term *Adam*. See *Yalkut Barmitzvah* (C'far Chabad: Kehos, 5745[1985]), p. 34, fn. 13.

CHAPTER 4

THE SPIRITUAL CLARIFICATION OF THE RECLAMATION OF FREUD

Freudian instincts and Divine attributes

Freud's work has attracted interest in its relationship to religious mysticism and specifically the teachings of the Kabbalah. A pioneering attempt to explore this connection was made by David Bakan, in his *Sigmund Freud and the Jewish Mystical Tradition*, first published in 1958. Joseph Berke's *The Hidden Freud – His Hassidic Roots* is a recent book in this genre. It follows Berke's own interest in synthesizing psychoanalysis with perspectives of his own traditional religious belief.

What is the affinity of Freud's theory with religious mysticism, that awakens the search for the roots of his psychoanalysis in religious tradition? Freud – unlike Frankl in relation to the Maharal of Prague – did not claim (to my knowledge) any religious lineage for his ideas. Simply to say that Freud had Jewish religious books, including a fundamental mystical work, the *Zohar* (in translation), in his library, and that his father and earlier forebears were Jewishly religiously observant, does not of itself seem to be enough to establish a connection.

These reasons are insufficient because traces of such background and contacts cannot overweigh the manifest and explicit hostility of Freud in his writings to religion, which he termed a "collective obsessional neurosis". G-d, soul and religion were not for him authentic reality, but simply the delusional content of a Superego imposed by civilization to repress instinct at the cost of personal happiness. His book *Civilization and its Discontents* seeks to lay bare traditional culture with its religious underpinnings as the opponent of human actualization. His *Moses and Monotheism* grossly reinvents historical Judaism in order to uphold his psychoanalytic theory.

The justifiable grounds for a search to relate Freud to religious – and particularly the mystical religious – tradition cannot therefore be found in Freud's conscious *intentions*. Rather, valid grounds exist in certain objective conceptual parallels of Freud's work with the mystical religious tradition, which those acquainted with the mystical religious tradition themselves notice. These parallels or similarities exist, notwithstanding Freud's professed hostility to religious tradition, and whether or not Freud, at any (but the deepest spiritually) unconscious level, was aware of them. By going to the source of the parallel concepts in religious tradition, we can delineate what is reclaimable – and under what transformation – for religious tradition. This is, of course, significant also for Frankl's ideal of a reclamation of Freud, as discussed in the last Chapter, since Frankl also identified the roots of his own thought in religious tradition.

The first point of comparison of Freudian theory with the mystical religious tradition is – surprising as it may sound on first hearing – between the religious teaching of the Divine attributes and the Freudian instincts. It is the mystical strain in the religious tradition from Sinai which contains a teaching of the G-dly attributes (which it terms *s'firos*). The attributes do not inhere in G-d Himself, Who is beyond all description. Rather, G-d created these attributes, with and through which He acts in creation. The soul of the human being is also created with these attributes (on a human scale) and so mirrors, or resonates with, the Divine attributes. Through actualization of these soul attributes in in ethical character and conduct the individual is able to imitate[1], and thereby to draw close to, the Divine.

The Divine attributes are ten in number, comprised of three "intellectual" attributes and seven "emotional" attributes. The intellectual attributes are "insight" (*chochma*), "analysis" (*bina*) and "understanding" (*da'as*). The seven emotional attributes, which shall concern us here, since they pertain particularly to the universal human Divine likeness (*Tzelem Elokim*), are: love (*chesed*), judgment or discipline (*g'vurah*), beauty or mercy (*tiferes*), endurance (*netzach*), humility (*hod*), bonding (*y'sod*) and kingship (*malchus*)[2]. It is with regard to

---

[1] To the extent that is humanly possible and *specifically* through the Divinely given laws which translate these attributes into human conduct, as Rashi cites the Sages in his commentary to Deuteronomy 11:22: "[G-d] is merciful and you should be merciful; He bestows kindness and you should bestow kindness".

[2] Some of these are the translations of the attributes found in Rabbi Simon Jacobson, *A Spiritual Guide to Counting the Omer*, NY: Vaad Hanochos Hatmimim, 1996.

these last seven attributes, that our comparison with the Freudian theory of the instincts is concerned.

The tradition from Sinai indicates that the seven Noahide laws correspond to the last-mentioned seven Divine attributes[3]. Accordingly, the same seven Divine attributes in the human soul prepare the human personality for an inner resonance with the conduct of the seven Noahide laws. In Chapter 2, we showed how the Maharal relates the Noahide laws to the spirit and structure (in Frankl's terms, the "dimensional ontology") of human personality in its personal and interpersonal spheres. The very same writing of the Maharal, however, *also* intimates the specific correspondence of the Noahide laws with the G-dly attributes.

This he does by elaborating upon a *Midrash*[4], which states that, with transgression of the distinct Noahide laws by successive generations of early humanity, the Divine presence withdrew from its manifestation upon earth, at the beginning of creation, stagewise back upwards through each of the "Seven Heavens"[5]. Thus, with the transgression by one generation of one of the Noahide laws (the law relating to the treatment of nature), the Divine presence left the earth and withdrew to the first Heaven; with the transgression by a subsequent generation of a second of the Noahide laws (the law prohibiting killing), it withdrew further to the second Heaven. In the mystical dimension, the significance of the Seven Heavens is that they represent successive embodiments of the seven emotive Divine attributes. Just as the fulfilment of the Seven Noahide Laws in their totality was requisite for the manifestation of the Divine Presence upon earth (as at the beginning of the Creation), so did their progressive and cumulative violation cause the Divine Presence progressively to retreat in ever greater spiritual distance from the earth. Once the Divine Presence had retreated to the seventh Heaven, seven great righteous figures in their successive generations, continues the *Midrash*, brought the Divine presence progressively back down to earth.

Thus, Abraham, who exemplified in his own character and conduct the Divine attribute of *chesed* (loving kindness) corrected in his generation the travesty of

[3] See Rabbi Menachem M. Schneerson in the discourse *"Zechor eis asher oso HaShem"* 5744 (1984).

[4] *Midrash Rabbo, Shir HaShirim* 5:1.

[5] The Seven Heavens are not the same as the celestial spheres (*galgalim*). See Maharal of Prague, *B'er HaGola, B'er HaShishi*. For the correlation of the Seven Heavens with the seven "emotive" s'firos, see Admur HaTzemach Tzedek, *Sefer HaChakira*, NY, Kehos, 2003 in *Hosofos*, p. 202.

the Noahide law of sexual morality (which relates to *chesed*). So he was able to draw down the Divine Presence one step (Heaven) closer to earth – from the Seventh Heaven (associated with *chesed*) to the Sixth Heaven. Isaac, his son, in the next generation, who exemplified the Divine attribute of *g'vurah* (associated with justice), rectified the travesty of the Noahide law of justice, bringing the Divine Presence another step closer to earth, from the Sixth Heaven (the domain of *g'vurah*) to the Fifth Heaven. Jacob, his son, who exemplified the Divine attribute of *tiferes* (mercy, compassion or beauty), rectified in his generation the travesty of the Noahide law prohibiting blasphemy (associated with the corruption of *tiferes*). So, he returned the Divine Presence from the Fifth Heaven (the place of *tiferes*) yet a step closer to earth, to the Fourth Heaven. And so it continued, generation after generation, through successive righteous figures (Levi, Kehos, Amram, until finally Moses) who rectified the travesties of the remaining Noahide laws, so that the Divine Presence returned to manifestation upon earth again in the generation of Moses.

Thus, (1) with the account of the Maharal, who states which Noahide law was rectified by *which* righteous individual (2) and the association of each of the seven spiritual Heavens and their corresponding specific Divine attributes with each of those seven righteous individuals, we can (3) find the correlation of the Noahide laws with the Divine attributes, as their practical expression in human conduct and law:

Biblical figure	Divine Attribute	Noahide law
Abraham	*Chesed*	Sexual morality
Isaac	*G'vurah*	Justice
Jacob	*Tiferes*	Reverence for G-d
Levi	*Netzach*	Prohibition of theft
Kehot	*Hod*	Prohibition of idolatry and belief in G-d
Amram	*Y'sod*	Prohibition of murder
Moses	*Malchus*	Treatment of animals (and nature)

We come now to the Freudian instincts. These in fact turn out to correspond to the Divine attributes, but in their *corrupted* forms. The Freudian instincts, with their associated "negative" behaviours, represent the raw, untutored "native" form of Divine attributes in human personality, *prior* to their refinement as an expression of the G-dly attributes. In Freudian terms, they operate as mere *drives* or *instincts*. The writings of the Maharal, moreover, show us how individual attributes, whether in their raw unrefined form as instincts, or in their state of refinement, relate to the elements of the structure of human personality.

We have seen, in Chapter 2, that the Maharal delineates four elements of human personality. The first three are the "faculties": (1) the physical or bodily dimension (2) the vital-intellectual dimension and (3) the unitive dimension, which provides the overall organization of the first two dimensions in the service of a particular meaning or purpose. Finally (4) there is a dimension which "comprises" and animates all the three faculties of personality: it is the soul, or the "Divine likeness" within the human. It acts (primarily from its principal place of residence in the higher unitive faculty) to prescribe refined moral qualities – attributes – as the content of each of the three faculties. Where it is suppressed or displaced, a contrary spirit – a coarse materiality – enters to produce the corruption of all the three faculties.

We now find, further, in writings of the Maharal (cited and footnoted at the beginning of Chapter 2) a correlation of the attributes, whether in their refined or raw form, with the three faculties and with the fourth – encompassing, orienting and animating – dimension, the soul or spirit, which orients all. The attribute of *chesed*, love or kindness, is associated with the physical-bodily dimension of personality. In its raw or degenerate form this is lust, corresponding to the Freudian Eros or libido of the Id. The attribute of *g"vurah*, judgment and discipline, is associated with the mental dimension. In its raw or degenerate form, it is punitive and harsh: corresponding to the Freudian *Thanatos* or aggressive instinct of the Ego. The attribute of *tiferes* (beauty, but also compassion) is associated with higher unitive faculty, which sanctifies and glorifies G-d, the source of all true meaning and morality. In its raw and degenerate form, it rebels against G-d, glorifying itself: corresponding to the Freudian *Narcissus* or the instinctual narcissism of the Superego. The fourth dimension – the soul itself – is associated with the attribute of *malchus*[6], kingship, for it derives its power, from the fact that it is utterly receptive, and given over, to the true and ultimate King, G-d himself. It has "nothing of its

---

[6] The last of the Divine attributes *malchus* itself takes root in a level, *kesser*, literally the "crown", transcending the Divine attributes themselves It is the profound self-abnegation or self-transcendence of *malchus* which enables it to receive from a qualitatively different (transcendent) realm of G-dliness *(kesser)*. Thus, it can function as "soul" vis-à-vis the faculties of the personality. See Rabbi M. M. Schneerson, *Likkutei Sichos*, Vol. 11, p. 61 and Vol. 23, p. 7, fn 38.

own": in Franklian terms, it is pure "self-transcendence" towards G-d. This attribute receives the template of the Divine attributes and "installs" them in the faculties of personality. Where the soul is repressed or displaced, another spirit – of gross and imperious self-absorption – enters. This contrary corrupted attribute of *malchus* – mere, driving instinctuality – is the animating spirit which installs within human personality the Freudian Eros, Thanatos and Narcissus: corrupted *chesed,* corrupted *g"vurah* and corrupted *tiferes.* The Divine attributes degenerate into mere instincts.

We have delineated the three Freudian instincts and the spirit of instinctuality itself, as the parallel, degenerate forms of the Divine spiritual attributes *chesed, g'vurah* and *tiferes* and *malchus* in the template of the soul. We have not sought (and perhaps there are not to be found) in Freud's psychoanalytic theory, instinctual correlates for the remaining attributes of *netzach, hod* and *y'sod.* Suffice it for us here to say that these three attributes are derivatives of the three primary attributes, as follows. *Netzach* is a derivative of *chesed.* The corresponding Noahide law for *netzach* is the prohibition of theft: the desire for money is a lust akin to sexual desire (controlled by the Noahide law of sexual morality in the attribute of *chesed*). *Hod* is a derivative of *g"vurah.* The Noahide law corresponding to *hod* is the prohibition of idolatry. Just as injustice (controlled by the Noahide law of justice in the attribute of *g"vurah*) is a perversion of intellect in arbitrating between claimants, so is idolatry a perversion of intellect in its absolutization of the relative, as Frankl would put it. Finally, *y'sod* is a derivative of *tiferes.* The Noahide law corresponding to *y'sod,* is the prohibition of killing. Just as the corruption of *tiferes* is blasphemy (controlled by the Noahide law against blasphemy) that is, rebellion against G-d, so is killing a striking against G-d – namely, against the Divine likeness stamped on the soul, which animates human life. The (inverted) parallels between the Divine attributes and the Freudian instincts in the structure of personality is set out in the following figure:

The intellectual faculty (in Freud: Ego)	The unitive faculty (in Freud: Superego)	The bodily faculty (in Freud: Id)
G'vurah (in Freud: aggression)		Chesed (in Freud: libido)
	Tiferes (in Freud: narcissisim)	
Hod		Netzach
	Yesod	
	Malchus	

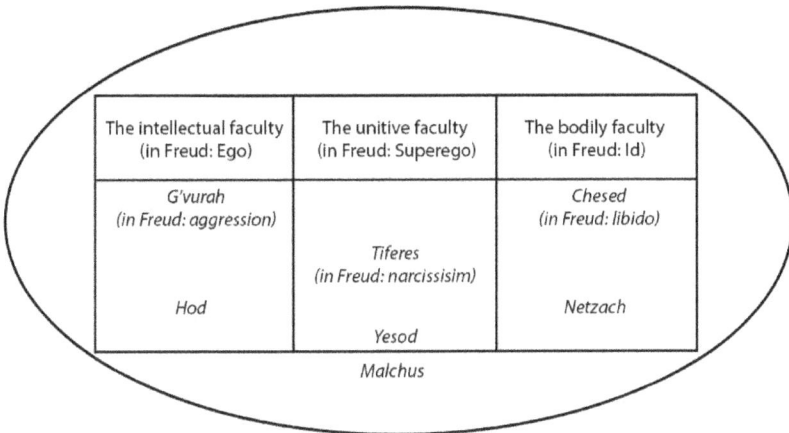

Paradoxically, from the standpoint of religious tradition what Freud has said about the human personality is *true* – but it is true of the *bad* facticity – the degenerate state, the unclean "basement" – of the human being. It is an inverted-mirror image of the Divine template of human personality. This provides a powerful insight into the reclamation of Freudian theory for psychotherapy: that it not only identify, but also modify and ultimately *transform*, the instincts.

Freud and the Grand Rabbi:
the transformation of instincts

That Freud himself could grasp a concept of the transformation of the instincts emerges from a highly significant encounter between Freud and a great religious leader. A meeting took place in Vienna in the European winter of 1902-03 between Freud and Rabbi Sholom DovBer Schneerson, a grand Rabbi ("Rebbe") of the Lubavitch Chassidic dynasty, who travelled to see Freud, in the company of his son, Rabbi Yosef Yitzchok Schneerson, who documented it. It is not clear whether the Rabbi came to see him on account of neurological issues (in relationship to a hand) or psychological ones, or both. No record of the meeting appears in Freud's psychoanalytical files[7]. This would tend to suggest that the Rabbi came to see Freud in his side-specialty, physical neurology. The meeting is recorded in a number of places in the published writings of Chabad Chassidic thought.

---

[7] According to enquiries made to the Freud archive. This could be because the consultation began, as was regarded by, Freud, as primarily a neurological – not a psychological – one. This follows the indication that the reason for the visit was neurological, as suggested in letters of the Rabbi at http://col.org.il/show_news.rtx?artID=55582#full. There is, however, a suggestion also of a psychological cause for the visit in the account of the visit in Rabbi M.M. Schneerson, *Reshimos*, (N.Y: Kehos) Vol. 5, *Choveres* 94.

The encounter had both a religious and psychological side. The Rabbi discussed the relationship of heart and mind with Freud, as taught in Chassidic teaching (Chassidus), as Rabbi Yosef Yitzchok Schneersohn relates:

> On account of his ill health, my father [Rabbi Sholom DovBer Schneersohn] had travelled to Vienna to consult one of the leading medical specialists there, and in order to arrive at a clear diagnosis this gentleman asked for the details of my father's daily program, including the hours he worked and the way his work was arranged. And when *Chassidus* was mentioned he wanted to know what kind of scholarly discipline this was.
>
> My father replied: "The discipline of *Chassidus* requires that the head explain the heart what the person should want, and that the heart implement in the person's life that which the head understands."
>
> "How can that be done?" asked the specialist. "Are head and heart not two continents separated by a vast ocean?"
>
> To this my father answered: "The task is to build a bridge that will span these two continents, or at least to connect them with telephone lines and electric wires so that the light of the head should reach the heart. As a result of various observations and discoveries, I must add that in those who are born into this branch of learning" – my father referred here to Chassidim –
>
> "the substance of the brain, in which their psychological and intellectual faculties reside, and the substance of the heart, have an innate aptitude for this branch of learning and for the tasks it demands."[8]

It would seem that the Rabbi also mentioned psychological issues of his own, as emerges from the account of the seventh Lubavitcher Rebbe, Rabbi Menachem Mendel Schneerson, who heard it from his father-in-law, Rabbi Yosef Yitzchok:

> In the year [56]63 *Admur nishmaso Eden* [a term referring to Rabbi Sholom DovBer] was suffering from low spirits. He did not relate much detail to me, but lamented a great deal before my mother…[His complaint was] that after years of *avodah* [(effort in the service of G-d), he felt that] not even one *middah*

---

[8] Rabbi Y. Y. Schneersohn, *Likkutei Diburim* (translated by Uri Kaploun), Vol. 1, N.Y.: Kehot, 1987, pp. 174-75.

[emotional attribute of his] was as it should be; and that all [his] intellectual comprehension was not clear to him and that he was not able to delve deeply into a[ny] concept [of Torah study or prayer].

This was notwithstanding the fact that all this happened in that winter, in which we saw how deeply engaged he was in his thoughts…and also after the [celebration of the] 19th of Kislev [a major festive day in the Chassidic calendar] of that year, which [year's celebration and his intellectual contribution to it] has won a special reputation of its own.

On account of this, we travelled that winter to Vienna to seek advice from doctors. [My father] visited Freud.[9]

In another account, Freud's explanation of the Rabbi's state was summarized by Rabbi Yosef Yitzchok in these terms:

The Professor stated that his [the Rebbe's] suffering was a deep, inward [one], which is [found] only in profound, committed thinkers. The heart desires more than the head can grasp, and the head understands more than the heart can come to.[10]

One aspect of the interchange between Freud and the Rabbi had to do with the relationship between heart and mind. The Rabbi pointed out to Freud, that the task of Chassidism is to inform, elevate and redirect emotion. This was clearly not something about which Freud was accustomed to hear, let alone himself speak – and in positive terms. Freud in much of his writings had spoken about religious experience and values, though not as virtues, but rather as sources of neurosis.

Yet here Freud was brought to an insight. He beheld and recognized a person, in whom emotion had not simply been subordinated to intellect such as to be in accordance with what the spiritually informed intellect requires. Rather he saw a level of refinement and depth of *emotion*, that even the spiritually attuned *intellect* does not possess. "The heart desires more than the head can comprehend": the heart has a purity of spiritual quest, which the mind cannot understand. Equally, Freud recognized that the refined mind, he beheld in the Rabbi, perceived things which the heart could not contain: "the head understands more than the heart can come to". In other words, he saw refined emotion standing in a relationship of equality with refined intellect, not because

---

[9] *Reshimos, loc. cit.*, Present author's translation.
[10] *Sefer HaSichos* 5701 (1941), C'far Chabad: Kehot, 1976, p. 28. Present author's translation.

they are the same, but because each has been independently transformed to actualize its own unique spiritual power.

Freud could have had little doubt that here he beheld a person in whom the spiritual – the soul – was in a state of manifestation and irradiation of the entire personality. But he chose to focus here on what Frankl calls the "psychophysical" dimension: intellect and emotion. Each of these faculties in the Rabbi had come into parity, each with a refinement and superiority of its own. Intellect had a reach of grasp and perception of the Divine which emotion could not hold ("contain"); and feeling had a quality of power and intensity of cleaving to the Divine, which intellect could not grasp. The "Id" and the "Ego" were both – separately and uniquely – transformed through and in their distinct relationships with the soul. The psychophysical self of Rabbi Sholom DovBer had been wholly refined. What then is the meaning of the "depression", which according to parts of the account, brought him to Freud?

Freud's analysis, that he here beheld an individual in which *"the heart desires more than the head can grasp, and the head understands more than the heart can come to"* answers the question.

When feeling and intellect have separately been refined to the highest degree, as they were in Rabbi Sholom DovBer, they *cannot be satisfied* by one another[11]. Each one, so to speak, is making a critique of the other. *From the standpoint of purified emotion,* no intellectual perception is true enough; the visceral demand of the heart for truth will not be satisfied by what the intellect can supply of that truth. Thus, the Rabbi had complained that his understanding lacked clarity, lucidity.

On the other hand – and this is the intellect's critique of feeling – an immensely honed spiritual intellect (as evinced by Rabbi Sholom DovBer's extraordinary corpus of writings and the account of the depth of his thought in that year) could comprehend wonders of G-dliness, which the cleaving of feeling could not match: "more than the heart can come to". It can perceive a majesty of G-dliness, for example, which should prompt, but cannot evoke, a corresponding intensity of feeling of awe. Since emotion cannot ascend to that plane of intellectual perception, it is felt from that perspective to be inadequate: "not even one *middah* was as it should be". The resultant depression was thus what might be deemed the "occupational hazard" of persons, whom Freud called "profound" and "committed", whose intellect and feeling had

---

[11] Note here also the commentary of the Maharal on *Avos* 4:14: as to why *Kehuna* and *Malchus* generally cannot both be present in the one person.

each been immensely refined. This, in other words, was the symptom, not of illness but, of greatness.

Freud's counsel to the Rabbi is also recorded:

[In counsel, Freud] instructed that his environment should be "pleasant": that they [the Chassidim] should learn his words [- teachings – carry out] his instructions and see to it that he was informed about [what they did in relation to] this – in order that through this they should lift up his spirits."[12]

Rabbi Menachem Mendel Schneerson explains the significance of Freud's response in the following terms:

[Following on from] that which was previously spoken about on *Lag B'Omer* with regard to the praises which the students of Rabbi Shimon bar Yochai [the great Mishnaic sage and author of the *Zohar*] gave him, it is ostensibly out of place that the righteous [should allow praise of themselves, this being inconsistent with their humility]. Nevertheless, we find that it is sometimes necessary to evoke something [in the righteous] through causing them pleasure, along the lines of the above [related] story about the doctor's [Freud's] instruction that he [Rabbi Sholom DovBer] be informed that they [the Chassidim] were learning, and were immersed in, his teaching[13].

Perhaps, one could suggest here a further explanation. Emotions are called "children" (*toldos* – derivatives) of intellect inasmuch as intellect has the power to engender emotions consistent with its understanding. Similarly, students (followers) are called "children" of their teachers in religious tradition. The relationship of emotion to intellect is thus in a sense played out in the relationship of teacher and students. He is their externalized mind and they are his externalized emotions. When, therefore, the Rabbe's followers (students) would study his teaching and *show* that they had understood it, this would in the Rebbe himself bring about a equilibrium, and mutual satisfaction of his heart and mind. For then "heart" (the students) had appreciated the "mind" (the Rebbe); and "mind" (the Rebbe) would find itself acknowledged, resonant

---

[12] Rabbi Menachem Mendel Schneerson, *Reshimos* 5758 (1998), N.Y: Kehot, *Parshas Behar*, 1998.

[13] Rabbi Menachem Mendel Schneersohn, *His'vadus* 5758 (1998), Transcript of address from the year 1962 (Parshas B'chukosai, 5722), published in N.Y: Kehot, 1998.

and affirmed in the "heart" (the students)[14]. Whether or not this last interpretation is correct, Freud, at all events, had glimpsed the transformation of instincts (whether of the emotion of the Id into *chesed* and the intellect of the Ego, into *g"vurah*) as purified and refined – we would say, G-dly – attributes.

Psychotherapeutic means for logotherapeutic-spiritual ends

How psychoanalysis can specifically be reworked as therapy to help with the modification and transformation of instincts (attributes) is, as mentioned, outside the scope of this study[15]. We can, however, consider how psychotherapy in *general* – of which psychoanalysis is a kind – needs to function in tandem with the spiritual norms located by logotherapy. The division of labour proposed by Frankl between logotherapy and psychotherapy is that logotherapy works with the human spirit and the principal residence of the human spirit, the noetic or meaning faculty, to find meaning, purpose and value. Psychotherapy, on the other hand, works with the somatic and the mental faculties, to align these with the purpose, meaning and value discovered by the individual with the help of logotherapy. The primary difference between the two is that the language of the noetic dimension and the human spirit is largely "rational". That is to say, it can be addressed through a discussion about values and belief and analysis of personal existence. The psychophysical dimension, on the other hand, often the home of insurgent feeling and distorted perception, is less, or not at all, amenable to rational, norm-related discourse.

There are exceptions in both cases. Sometimes the "rational" noetic faculty

---

[14] See the development of this possible further explanation in the postscript of the revised version of the "The Encounter of the Rebbe RaShaB and Freud" published as a free-standing booklet by the Institute for Judaism and Civilization, Melbourne, 2010. The earlier version is found in "The encounter of Freud and the fifth Lubavitcher Rebbe" in the *Journal of Judaism and Civilization*, Vol. 2 (1999). The postscript builds on the contribution to that article by Dr Edwin Harari, who refers to the "object-relations" theory developed by Freud's student, Melanie Klein within the psychoanalytic tradition.

[15] Joseph Berke suggests that Melanie Klein's object-relations theory may have a role to play here in that she speaks of the child's needs for "containers" to repair the chaos of primary interests. Berke writes, "...when a child is born, the unity between the child and his mother is broken. Then the child struggles to contain the primary impulses, which Freud called Eros and Thanatos, and which Klein recognized as the Life Impulse and the Death Impulse" (*The Hidden Freud*, London: Karnac, 2015, p. 44). He associates the reparative motif in Klein's work with the Kabbalistic doctrine of the "breaking of the vessels," which had previously held the light of the Divine attributes, and the process of reparation needed to repair them so as again to house sanctity within the creation. This cosmic process of breakage and repair in the "world", at large, is paralleled in the human psyche (*Ibid.*, pp. 155-56).

must itself be stimulated and opened to self-transcendence – that is to say, to elicitation of the human spirit or soul or conscience – through non-rational techniques. An example of this is "paradoxical intention", a method developed by Frankl, to which we have already referred. Conversely, a spiritual appeal can sometimes be made in the psychophysical realm, where there operates a residue of the human spirit that, in Frankl's words, never becomes sick and retains the power of decision. It can and must use its leverage even in the sub-rational recesses of personality. We examined instances of this from Frankl's accounts in Chapter 1. Nevertheless, the basic division of labour – between the normative discourse of logotherapy and the practical techniques of psycho-therapy – remains. Their cooperation consists in the use of psychotherapeutic means need to serve the moral and meaning ends of logotherapy.

Frankl put it this way with regard to the logotherapeutic employment of a modified Freudian psychoanalysis:

> According to a statement once made by Sigmund Freud, psy-choanalysis rests on the recognition of two concepts, repression as the cause of neurosis and transference as its cure. Whoever believes in the importance of these two concepts, may justifiably regard and call himself a psychoanalyst.
>
> Repression is counteracted by growing awareness. Repressed material should be made conscious. Or, as Freud put it, where id had been ego should become. Freed from the mechanistic ideology of the nineteenth century, seen in the light of the exis-tentialist philosophy of the twentieth century, one could say that psychoanalysis promotes self-understanding in man.
>
> Similarly, the concept of transference can be refined and purged…Freed from its manipulative quality, transference could be understood as a vehicle of that human and personal encounter which is based on the I-Thou relation. As a matter of fact, if self-understanding is to be reached, it has to be medi-ated by encounter. In other words, Freud's statement, where id is, ego should be, could be enlarged: Where id is, ego should be; but the ego can become an ego only through a Thou.[16]

My understanding of this passage is that for a suitably modified and appropri-ated psychoanalysis (a psychotherapy) to do its work with psychophysical (the id-ego) self, this psychodynamic method must itself be oriented. Its orientation

---

[16] *The Will to Meaning*, pp. 11-12.

is through the "Thou", namely, that to which the human is called to transcend for meaning, purpose and value. The work of the psychotherapist must operate under the aegis of self-transcending meanings and values accomplished ("mediated") through the logotherapeutic encounter. The logotherapist and psychotherapist need not be two separate people. Indeed, it may be impractical for this to be the case; rather they can function in the same person. The two (logotherapeutic and psychotherapeutic) functions, however, must be distinguished and yet coordinated.

Logotherapy, in a spiritual perspective, requires that every behaviour be evaluated in meaning or moral terms. Does a person's bodily emotion reflect a valid moral purpose and orientation – is it a moral sexuality for example? Is a perception sanctionable by reference to healthy moral conscience – is it caught up for example in an irrational fear, which discloses a false view of the world? Is the world-view of an individual reasonable or pathological, an expression of what Frankl called a "collective neurosis"? Every behaviour in other words is evaluated in terms of its meaning and moral Gestalt (form). Psychotherapy then enters to work with the non-rational, non-spiritual recesses of personality, be it with medication, hypnosis or any other of a host of psychotherapeutic techniques. Logotherapy addresses the higher "human" self. Psychotherapy works with the lower, psychophysical self to bring it into consonance with the norms and meanings set for it by the applicable norms discovered by the higher self.

A cursory glance at, to take an example, Jewish religious literature on psychotherapy reveals these different aspects of the composite relationship of psychotherapeutic technique and spiritual-ethical norm. Rabbi A. Amsel, in *Judaism and Psychology*[17] and in *Rational Irrational Man*[18], posits the principle that "there is basically no difference in kind between the dynamics of normal and abnormal behaviour, the difference being of degree only" and "Judaism views mental illness as a moral rather than a medical problem. It is only where communication with the patient is impossible that Judaism would assign the cure to the medical profession", by which he presumably means the interventions of psychotherapy[19]. Where rational and moral communication is possible, the task of psychology is the "re-education" of the character qualities *(middos)* of the patient with reference to normative concepts, in this case, in Judaism.

---

[17] N.Y: Feldheim, 1969.

[18] N.Y: Feldheim, 1976.

[19] *Rational Irrational Man*, pp. 6-7.

The problem, acknowledged by Rabbi Amsell, is that one of the hallmarks of many forms of mental illness is itself the loss of rational self-perception; then it is difficult or inappropriate for therapy to be carried out at the level of rational moral discourse. There is a non-rational realm which does *not readily* listen to reason.

One finds, then, the approach of Rabbi Chaim Lipshitz as epitomized in the final sentence of an interview: "I tend towards careful use of psychological techniques and not the philosophy behind them"[20]. This approach, whilst professing a concern to avoid the psychotherapeutic affirmation of questionable norms, seeks out an application of clinical technique "freed" of normative questions. Ostensibly, normative considerations, guiding the ends (in terms of desired behaviours) and the means (how, when and where one may apply a technique) are inescapable. Just as we are not dealing with disembodied reason, so too, human beings – the patient and the therapist – work in the context of meanings and values. He does not ignore this question by qualifying his approach as "the *careful* use of psychological techniques".

A third view, questing the ideal of "scientifically won" therapeutic practices *united with* Divinely given law *(halachah)*, is found in the writings of Moshe Halevi Spero[21]. Spero favours what he terms a "unified halachic view"[22], which, however, seeks to determine the foundations *in religious law itself* for specific clinical treatments. This is a profound ideal, but the problem is whether adequate psychotherapeutic methods will practically be discovered by the therapist in the pure realm of religious law. An approach, which indeed unifies halachic-normative and scientific-empirical dimensions (a "unified halachic [psychotherapeutic] view") is a utopian – but not for that reason invalid – desideratum. In a spiritually repaired world and human psyche, in which the psychophysical dimension is *actually united* with the spiritual (housed in the noetic realm) the desideratum has its place. On the other hand, in the spiritually damaged world (which includes damaged psyches) in which the spiritual and psychophysical realms have been sundered, empirical methods must be employed which *work* – not necessarily for reasons which can be discovered in religious law. If psychotherapeutic technique and normative discourse (here,

---

[20] In the journal *T'chumim* 5740, Vol. 1, p. 279.

[21] *Judaism and Psychology – Halakhic Perspectives*, Ktav-Yeshivah University Press: N.Y., 1980 and *Handbook of Psychotherapy and Jewish Ethics*, Jerusalem: Feldheim, 1986.

[22] Psychology as Halakhah: Toward a Halakhic Metapsychology" in *Judaism and Psychology – Halakhic Perspectives*.

logotherapy) must remain separate, as they are in a "damaged" world, they can still be brought together. This is when psychotherapeutic means are distinguished from logotherapeutic ends and yet are brought to serve them.

These notes, on the practice of empirical psychotherapy yoked to spiritual or normative values of personality, relate to any psychotherapy, not simply psychoanalysis. But what for Frankl made this psychotherapy – Freudian psychoanalysis – an incomparable psychotherapy ("no one will ever be able to measure up to him")?

Aside from his recognition of the genius of Freud (however much Frankl thought his "theoretical assumptions" required correction), I believe that the answer to this question lies in the deep – perhaps "unconscious" – spiritual affinity between the two great psychologists. The "roots" of Frankl's theory are consciously spiritual and those of Freud's theory are, to borrow Berke's word, "hiddenly" so. Frankl grasped the system of the faculties of human personality through the template of mind as an "ontological dimensionality" properly oriented through self-transcendence. Freud grasped the system of the faculties of personality through the template of emotion as a dynamic system of instincts (in spiritual terms, "attributes"). Both of these perspectives cohere in the religious tradition from Sinai, in Frankl's words, the "higher" dimension, "inclusive" of psychology. It is the religious tradition that teaches about the soul, which is the fount of psyche and the structurer and unifier of heart and mind. Accordingly, the teaching of this tradition can clarify and bring together the truths in both Frankl and Freud.

CHAPTER 5

THE TRADITION THAT BRINGS
FRANKL AND FREUD TOGETHER

The recovery of the soul

The significance of the religious tradition – which presents the "higher" dimension "including" the psychological reality of the human being, as Frankl put it – for psychology is that it supplies the ultimate and essential parameters of psychology itself[1]. It does this primarily through its teaching concerning

---

[1] Psychology is arguably the "primary" science in the sense that it sets out the conditions of knowledge as the activity of the human "knower", a human personality. For those who, like Georg Wilhelm Friedrich Hegel, are concerned with a philosophical or conceptual ordering of the sciences, there is accordingly strong reason to give the first place to psychology. This view is at variance with that of Hegel himself in his *Encyclopaedia of the Philosophical Sciences*, who gave "logic" that position. The reason for arguing against Hegel's choice is the insight that the activity of "knowing" (which produces the "sciences") involves an interaction of human faculties. What we customarily refer to as the analytic, reflective, thinking self ("mind", "intellect" or in psychoanalytic terms, the "ego") interacts with an immediately experiential self (the somatic, sentient self or "id") and with a higher meaning or values-framework self (the "noetic" faculty to use Frankl's term or "superego" to use Freud's). "Thought" or "science" is not simply a product of analysis, but also of a sentient relationship to objects in the world. These two functions are in turn organized by a comprehensive, value-structured outlook on things. All of these elements play into the activity of knowing.

The roles in "knowing" of the elements of psyche are replicated in the structure of science or knowledge itself. "Feeling", or to use a more old-fashioned term, "sensibility", in psyche corresponds in science to the "data" received through the physical senses. The function of "mind" is analogous in science to the analysis and construal of relationships or "laws" within the data. The "noetic", meaning dimension in personality corresponds in science to the general theoretical frameworks, which organize a range of individual "laws" in the light of a comprehensive view or paradigm. This threefold structure of knowledge is presented in the thought of Pierre Duhem. For a presentation of Duhem's thought see J. A. Schuster, "Pierre Duhem's History and Philosophy of Science in Contemporary

the human soul, which, as the rightful occupant of the noetic faculty, is also the organizer of the bodily and mental faculties of personality. As such the religious tradition sets out not only the "metaphysics" of what human personality ultimately is: mind, body and soul. It teaches also the "ethics" of human personality, namely, how the human personality should be: the concepts and content of normativity and aberration, of function and dysfunction. This has to do, in significant part with the extent to which the soul is active in deploying its normative review of thought and emotion in the mental and bodily dimensions of personality.

Even if psychology sets out initially to help the distressed personality, it can never heal mental ill-health without a model of the healthy personality. A psychiatrist friend of mine once told me, psychiatrists work in the "mud-patch" of human personality. Freud is quoted as having said that his work was in the "basement" of human personality[2]. The psychologically unwell person is a pathological variation of what the psychologically well person is and is diagnosed and healed in terms of a norm. Psychology explicitly or implicitly sets out a norm of "wellness".

Thus, "emotional" and "mental-perceptual" wellness are as much a norm as "noetic" wellness, and the soul requires them all. The soul is known in religious tradition as the "Divine likeness" and it implements the "imitation of the Divine" in all the faculties of personality. Frankl embraced the human soul, with its imitation of the Divine as the *ultimate* discovery of the human. Freud, we have seen, fought it, but in the event his theory can be reclaimed for the very same – indeed, *enhanced* – discovery. When the soul is conscious and has achieved its imprint in the human being, the human being has been "discovered".

The unique language of the soul, as distinct from that of mind (perception, thought) and body (emotion, feeling) is self-abnegation and the desire to cleave to G-d, for the sake of this alone. The "act" of the soul, or of faith, is thus in essence the "suspension" of both feeling and thinking in the quest to

---

Perspective", *Journal of Judaism and Civilization*, Vol. 12 (2017). The concept of "paradigm" derives from the work of Thomas Kuhn, also discussed in that article. The same threefold structure of knowledge, is known in Hegelian terms, as that of "subject", the analytic, determining mind; "object", the data of reality encountered by the subject; and the third element, "concept" which structurally and "dialectically" integrates subject and object.

[2] Frankl writes: 'In a letter to Ludwig Binswanger he [Freud] said himself: "I have always confined myself to the ground floor and basement of the edifice" called man', *The Will to Meaning*, p. 10. The term has already been cited in Chapters 3 and 4 of this Introduction.

identify with the Divine will. This does not mean that the attachment to G-d is without feeling or understanding. To the contrary. Rather, the soul must first cleave to G-d in order to imitate G-d. The soul is in essence ready to *do*, before it feels or thinks. From that self-commitment it "fetches" the template of G-dly (ethical) feeling and G-dly (ethical) thinking. In other words, it "returns" with this template to enclothe itself in both thought and feeling and to purify thought and feeling. Its language is that of Divine law – the Noahide laws – which properly and ethically structure thought and feeling, mind and body. Where this order is not followed, and is reversed, spontaneous feeling and spontaneous thought become the authors of morality and the moral compass of personality. Such feeling and thought, as we have seen especially in contemporary culture, can be deeply corrupted.

It is the religious tradition – the dimension, inclusive of psychology – which ensures that the human personality is given a soul. In the remainder of this section, we speak (1) briefly of the struggle in contemporary society and psychology for the soul, which is accomplished only by cognizance of the higher religious dimension and its tradition. In the second section of this Chapter, we recapitulate (2) how the religious tradition, particularly through the work of the Maharal of Prague can integrate both logotherapy and a revalued Freudian psychotherapy: how, in other words, the soul can imprint itself in both body ("heart") and mind. In the third section we see how (3) the religious tradition conceptualizes progressive levels at which the soul does imprint itself on heart and mind.

Just as religious tradition with its teaching of the soul informed Frankl's logotherapy, so conversely, does much of contemporary culture – with its "mainstream" psychology – reject the soul. The secularism of contemporary society is not simply the product of indifference, ignorance or lack of interest in the soul. It has tended to be "doctrinaire" in its secularism and rejection of the soul.

Doctrinairely secularist world-views – and especially the psychological theories and practices in which those world-views are embedded – actually function as ideologies to submerge the spiritual within the human. For the doctrinaire secularist, personality may thus be driven, at the "lower" end, by rudimentary desires or mere self-perceptions, or, at the "higher end" through the interests-structure of secular world-views. This is in accordance with the great secular sociologist Max Weber who understood world-views as "world images" serving as "channels along which action is moved by the dynamics of interests"[3]. Weber applied this definition to religions themselves for he himself could not "hear" the spiritual and so distinguish it (in essence) from materialistic world-views: by his own admission he was "religiously tone-deaf" *(religiös unmusikalish)*. In this, he was mistaken. Authentic religion, just like the soul, has no "interests" of its own. Rather, it is the transcendence of interests. Interests intrude from the "world" and from the "person" only once the soul – the transcender of interests – has been shut out. The soul is the experience of the creaturely human being drawn towards the will of the Creator.

Weber's concept of the world-view as a "dynamic of interests", accordingly applies to the ideological usurpers of the soul in the noetic faculty. They – not religion, as Freud would have it – are expressions of what Frankl called a "collective neurosis". I have called the doctrinaire secularism of the present age, which has eclipsed the human soul and G-d, the world-view of "hedonistic materialism"[4]. It has made the gratification of pleasure and the virtually unconditional flight from pain and the validation of morphing self-perception – psychophysical prompts – into the bases of a world-view.

For many species of doctrinaire secularism, freedom has been understood as freedom *from* a transcendent spiritual authority which posits objective, universal values. This purported freedom in fact reduces to a freedom to choose *amongst* interests: predispositions, impulses and perceptions, all arising from *within* psyche and culture. The essential and radical freedom, to which Frankl, along with religious tradition points, is to rise above interest *per se*. That comes about through active self-transcendence, through relativization of all interests which arise within the immanent worldly realm. So it is able to discriminate between valid and invalid interests: between those which are consonant with a Divine moral template and those which are not – to be able to answer the question "not, what do I want of life, but, what does life wants of me?"

This freedom as actualization of the sovereignty of the soul within the person, does not simply signify the repression of the "interests" of body, mind and cultural contents of the noetic faculty. Particular human needs, feelings, sensitivities, talents, life opportunities and cultural experiences are real and may have value in the life of the individual. The goal is rather, as stated, to

---

[3] Quoted in G. Roth and W. Schluchter, *Max Weber's Vision of History – Ethics and Methods*, cited above p. 21, fn 4.

[4] See S. D. Cowen, *Politics and Universal Ethics*, Ballan: Connor Court Publishing, 2011, Chapter 1.

adjudicate amongst, refine and revise, interests such that they align the person as, where and when he or she individually stands and has "become", with objective, Divine will.

This couples freedom with responsibility. One could think that the soul's *freedom* ultimately consists in breaking the fetters of all worldly and personal interests. Here, human *responsibility* reminds one of the obligation to "return" to the material self and the material "world", honing faculties and reconstructing interests such as to become an ethical agent in the world *with* those faculties and *amidst* those interests.

The soul's expression in heart and mind

Once the soul has been recovered and its sovereignty asserted within the human being, it "speaks" differently in each of the noetic, mental and somatic faculties of personality. Enthroned in the noetic faculty, the soul speaks in its essential voice and modality *as soul*. This essential aspect of the soul finds itself in the act of faith. Whilst many may experience G-d through feeling or intellect, this is so because the soul has *already* tutored feeling or intellect in this direction. In their "raw" state or, alternatively, as moulded by cultures alien to the spirit, feeling and intellect cannot be relied upon by themselves to "intend" towards the Divine. The experience and consciousness of the soul is nurtured by religious tradition. There is perhaps no more enduring experience and knowledge, notwithstanding the vicissitudes in the standing of faith, in history than the experiencing and knowing of the soul. We can say that the soul knows G-d and itself in a supra-sensible and supra-rational way. Their existence is *ratified* by the soul because their existence cannot be conclusively *scientifically* proven. The soul cannot be seen under a microscope, nor can G-d be seen through a telescope. Neither is in the plane of physical nature and phenomena, which the worldly sciences address. The soul itself has its own unique way of "knowing", which has been metaphorically likened to "seeing". The soul, having "seen", can then make its vision known to both understanding ("mind") and feeling ("body"). The soul exists within every human being. It is the Divine likeness in which the biblical verse states that the human – every human being – was fashioned. In some it is conscious; in others it is repressed and there are many degrees of its repression and expression.

The sovereign soul finds itself and G-d, Frankl indicates, through the act of faith. Frankl, following Pascal, calls belief a "wager":

> I do not think that belief is a form of thinking, a mental act, which has a diminished[, an inferior,] reality. To the contrary,

belief is thinking, which gains in reality through the existential position of the one thinking it. This certainly does not mean that belief is not-knowing. Rather, it means really that the act of believing is founded on an existential act. Blaise Pascal expressed the wager, or logical indeterminacy, of belief as follows. I can never *know* (logically) whether there is an ultimate meaning (G-d)...It is therefore not as a result of logical reasoning – because it cannot be out of mere lines of logical reasoning – that one comes to this decision. Rather one comes to this decision out of the depths of one's own being[5].

Frankl here does not use the term "wager" in the sense of a "bet" in a game of chance. It is a wager in the sense that it suspends, and proceeds independently of, intellectual calculation. It suspends intellect because intellect is in, of and by itself underequipped to attach one to G-d, just as emotion cannot by itself reliably "feel" its way to G-d. The certitude, courage and steadiness of faith proceeds rather from "the depths of one's own being", the actual experienced affinity with G-d, which the soul natively possesses[6]. In the act of faith the soul recognizes what it already knows: the transcendent "You" of G-d:

Behind the higher self (*Über-Ich*) of the human... stands the You of G-d. For the conscience could never decree immanently [within the person], were it not for the experienced You (*Du-Wort*) of transcendence.[7]

Characteristic of the soul's relationship to G-d (conditional upon neither understanding or feeling) is its preparedness to act, to *do* the will of G-d:

It is life, that places us before life's questions – which we have to answer. This answering is an answering for which we are responsible. That means, we answer the question about the purpose of life, in that we take responsibility for our lives. We cannot answer it with words, but ultimately only in deed[8].

The deed that connects the soul to G-d is the ethical imperative or commandment, the ethical Divine law, as applied to our each and every situation

---

[5] "The Science of the Soul", below p. 144.

[6] As Frankl quotes Pascal, "I would not have sought YOU, had I not already found YOU." "Time and Responsibility", below p. 108.

[7] *Der unbewusste G-tt*, p. 85. Present author's translation. This paragraph was not translated by Frankl in the English version, *The Unconscious G-d*.

[8] "The Science of the Soul", below p. 145.

calling for ethical response[9.]

The soul (or to use its secular name, the conscience) thus has objective ethical content. Sensing this, some secular psychology has come up with various models of "objective" religious consciousness, such as the set of cultural archetypes posited by C. G. Jung. This model was critiqued by Frankl as presenting an archaic fiction in place of the living reality of religious tradition. Another attempt has been made by Roberto Assagioli develop a concept of a "collective unconscious" in the concept of a collective or transpersonal collective higher self. Here, Frankl's criticism of Jung applies: why must one invent a collective spiritual consciousness when it already exists in the history of the soul – in the traditions of the great world religions?[10] The human soul expresses its inner make-up in the core, shared beliefs of the great world religious traditions. In Frankl's words, spirituality without this traditional, historical pedigree and specific content is simply illiterate, inchoate and inarticulate (sprachos):

> ...a person, without traditional religious affiliation would be none other than one who has no language. For religious language in general and for the average person is *only that of tradition-bound religious affiliation or it is nothing*.[11]

He also uses the artistic metaphor of perspectival lines in a painting which converge to a common point. So too the "lines" of universal, objective values all converge to a

> uniform point...this One, which unites all values. And perhaps the principal Jewish prayer which consists of six words and states that the one G-d is the only one – in its deepest and ultimate meaning can be interpreted in this sense[12].

These words were stated by G-d as part of the revelation at Mount Sinai and are emblematic of that revelation. The revelation, written down in the Pentateuch, contains both the laws given at Sinai and those given to all humanity, known as the "Noahide" laws, to which we have made frequent reference.

---

[9] We have noted that Frankl speaks of the refraction of the ethical commandments in the multitude of individual circumstances, which aligns the response of the attuned individual to the Divine will (or the "call of transcendence"). He writes, "Every situation is distinguished by its uniqueness and there is only one right answer to the problem posed by the situation at hand" *Man's Search for Meaning*, London: Rider, 2011 printing, pp. 62-63.

[10] "Ten Theses concerning the 'Person'", below p. 123.

[11] "Time and Responsibility", below p. 112.

[12] *Ibid.*, below pp. 109-10.

They represent the ethical will of G-d for creation, and hence they represent the ethical will of the human soul, made in G-d's likeness. The essence of soul resonates with the Divine will in its commitment to ethical deed.

The soul, as given over entirely to G-d, directs the human being away from self "to" G-d, but then, as we have noted, "returns" to integrate the faculties of personality in the service of G-d. Law, ethical will, is the unique province of the soul itself, but it shapes the subordinate faculties of feeling (soma, id) and intellect (mind, ego) consistently with that ethical will. Today, as throughout history, we hear a clamour about righteous "feelings", and intellectually apprized "rights" or "duties", which are invoked to justify conduct which is at variance with universal law and ethics. All we can say from the standpoint of the tradition from Sinai is that many of these are corrupted emotions and false intellections. The conduct of universal ethics and law is associated with – or rather produces – purified emotions and righted intellect. The soul teaches the mind how to think and the heart how to feel, though individual minds and hearts will also bring their unique strengths and modalities to the tuition which they can receive from the soul.

How then does the soul – which expresses itself in the commitment to ethical deed, to Divine will – imprint itself in the subordinate faculties of thought and feeling? Here the religious tradition demonstrates the answers to these questions through its clarification of logotherapy and a reclaimed Freudian psychoanalytic psychotherapy. The primary perspective of Frankl on personality as a whole (that is, on all its faculties) is through the lens of *intellect*. His hallmark concept of self-transcendence, applied to all the faculties, is primarily grasped by Frankl through intellect. The primary perspective of Freud on all the faculties of personality through the lens of *emotion*: personality is a system of instincts. The religious tradition, exemplified here through the work of the Maharal of Prague is able to interpret both Frankl and a (reclaimed) Freud, as harmonious and complementary with one another and with the soul – as follows.

For Frankl, the three faculties of personality – somatic, mental and noetic – in their integration are glimpsed through a primarily *philosophical* psychology, a "dimensional ontology" of personality. Frankl's own unique contribution to psychology was logotherapy, which took as its therapeutic instrument, a philosophical "existential *analysis*" With the concept of self-transcendence, logotherapy helps the individual open each faculty of personality, in the predicaments which face them, to higher "meanings" and "values" for actualization.

Here, we saw in Chapter 2 of this Introduction, that the Maharal also provided a template for the intellectual "take" on personality as a matrix generated out of the dimensions of personality (body, mind and unitive-noetic faculties) in the twin personal and interpersonal dimensions of human existence. The Maharal's *philosophical* model of personality is the spiritually clarified version of Frankl's dimensional ontology. It shows moreover, how the Franklian dimensional ontology of personality – interpreted through the intellectually conceived concept of self-transcendence – aligns with the values of the Noahide laws. The soul, which in essence is the imitation of G-d through commitment to the deed of the Noahide laws, so delivers its imprint for mind, in a language or template of mind.

The religious tradition, represented in the work of the Maharal of Prague, also demonstrates how *emotion* is drawn into alignment with soul. This emerges from the reconstruction or reclamation of the Freudian theory of the instincts through the correlation of the Divine attributes and the *redeemed or transformed* Freudian instincts. This was discussed was discussed at length in Chapter 4 of the Introduction. Thus, Freud's fundamentally emotive *(instinctual)* perspective on personality situates major instincts in the different faculties of personality: the Id with Eros, the Ego with Thanatos and the Superego with Narcissus. The project of grasping the structure of human personality also as an organization attributes – whether in corrupted or purified form – is accomplished with the help of the Maharal. The Maharal also sets out the equation of the distinct attributes with the faculties of human personality. In addition to this the Maharal also intimates the correlation of the attributes with the individual Noahide laws. Here then the emotional "take" or perspective on all the faculties of personality – a spiritual reconstruction of the Freudian theory of instincts – renders the soul's imprint in the language and template of emotion.

In summary, just as the Maharal brings the human personality through the lens of intellect – through a spiritually clarified logotherapy – into apposition with the soul, that is to say with the Noahide laws; so does he bring human personality through the lens of emotion – through a spiritually clarified reclamation of the Freudian theory of the instincts – into apposition with the soul, and its ethical will, the Noahide laws. The religious tradition shows us how the soul speaks in and through the language of intellect in the spiritual clarification of logotherapy. It shows how the souls speaks the language of the heart, emotion in the spiritually clarified revaluation of the Freudian theory of the instincts. In short, the religious tradition, the teacher of and about the soul, brings Frankl and Freud together.

The foregoing can be summarized in the following chart. In each case it is a distinct teaching of the Maharal, representative of the religious tradition, which brings the noetic faculty, mind and body into apposition with the soul, and its ethical template, the universal ethics of the Noahide laws.

Teachings of the religious tradition	Primary perspective on faculties of personality	Relationship to the Noahide laws
The religious teaching of the soul as "likeness" and imitation of the Divine	Noetic faculty/ Superego/Spiritual	The soul's expression as "imitation of G-d" through fulfilment of the Noahide laws
The spiritual clarification through the Maharal of Viktor Frankl's logotherapy (dimensional ontology with self-transcendence)	Mental faculty/ Ego / Intellectual	The matrix of personality ("Dimensional Ontology"), oriented towards self-transcendence, in congruence with the Noahide laws
The spiritual clarification through the Maharal of the reclamation of Sigmund Freud's theory of instincts	Bodily-somatic faculty/ Id / emotional	The faculties of human personality as a structure of "instincts" or attributes congruent, in their refined form, with the Noahide laws

Levels in the integration of heart and mind with the soul

The religious tradition explains that once the soul has taken up residence within the noetic faculty of the human being, it not only influences and crafts body ("heart") and mind in the "imitation of the G-d"; but also *binds them together* in different ways in this service. There are two modalities or "levels" in the unification of intellect and emotion with the soul. The first of these is where the intellect, *receiving the influence of the soul* then *works upon the heart*, the bodily-emotional complex. Rabbi M. M. Schneerson puts it this way:

> Intellect affects emotion. Once one understands with one's intellect the greatness of G-d...there has to be the additional

endeavour to engender [correspondingly fitting] emotions within the heart. The intellect has to occupy itself in enclothing itself in the world of feeling[13].

There is, however, also a second form of unification,

...connected with the *essence* of the soul, which operates auto-matically [–that is to say, without the intermediary engagement of the intellect described above–] such that the person cleaves with all one's being [to the soul's perception of G-d] such that feelings are drawn automatically into correspondence with that perception[14].

That is to say, in the second level, the soul works directly upon emotion, not via intellect (which it separately influences). In the first level, the soul works upon intellect, which in turn works, with what it has received from the soul, upon emotion.

These two levels in the soul's orientation of heart and mind to G-d are sequential in personal development, the second being higher than, and fol-lowing upon, the first. In the first, emotion follows intellect, which follows the soul. Emotion is disciplined and controlled – *checked* – by intellect. In the second level, emotion stands on a level, not less than, and not subordinate to, intellect. In the second level, the result of the direct nexus between the soul and emotion, is that emotion can be *transformed*, reaching heights that it does not achieve through its tutelage to intellect at the first level, where it was simply controlled.

These two levels in the integration of human personality – the soul's imitation of the Divine, accomplished in thought and feeling, are aligned in psycho-logical terms with the work of Frankl and the revalued and reclaimed – the "transformed" – Freud respectively. This has already been intimated in the preceding chapters of this Introduction. Yet these two models of personality integration emerge with fresh clarity through the relationships of Frankl and Freud to two great "Grand Rabbis" within the Chassidic strand of Jewish orthodoxy. These have already been partially discussed; we revisit them here to highlight these points.

The interaction of the seventh Lubavitcher Rabbi, Rabbi Menachem Mendel Schneerson, with Frankl followed historically the encounter of the fifth Lubavitcher Rabbi, Rabbi Sholom DovBer Schneersohn, with Freud.

---

[13] *Likkutei Sichos*, Vol. 39, p. 28.

[14] *Ibid.*, emphasis added.

Nevertheless, we shall discuss them in reverse order. Indeed, the encounter of Rabbi Sholom DovBer Schneersohn with Freud became *known* later[15]. But the stronger reason for reversing their order is that, conceptually, in spiritual terms, as mentioned, they bring out progressive levels: the level of personality integration represented by Frankl's work, brought out in the seventh Lubavitcher Rabbi's engagement with him, precedes the higher level of personality integration adumbrated in Freud's encounter with the fifth Lubavitcher Rabbi.

The involvement of Rabbi Menachem Mendel Schneerson, with Frankl – after the Second World War – had both intellectual and personal dimensions. The Rabbi had read and recommended Frankl's work to others. On a personal level, he sent an individual, who was travelling from New York (where the Rabbi resided) to Vienna to be his emissary in conveying a message to Frankl, who lived in Vienna. It turned out that when the visitor arrived at Frankl's door, Frankl had just penned (though not dispatched) his resignation[16] from the University of Vienna. This was the culmination of Frankl's despair at the derision of, or at least disinterest in, his work – in the academic heyday of Freudian psychoanalysis – by colleagues and students. The message which the visitor brought to Frankl from the Rabbi at this crucial moment was not to give up his work. Frankl was profoundly impacted by the personal message and the letter of resignation was not dispatched. As Frankl later acknowledged, the Rabbi had bolstered him at a critical moment. Frankl continued with his work, eventually to have a global impact.

On an intellectual and professional level, the work of Victor Frankl was commended, in a letter written by the Seventh Lubavitcher Rabbi to an individual, in the following terms:

> …the dynamics of [mental] health … demonstrate (if we need
> a demonstration for this) how powerful faith – particularly that
> [faith] which is connected with and expressed through concrete
> deed, communal involvement, fulfillment of *mitzvos* [Divine
> commandments] and so forth – is in regard to the basis of the

---

[15] The identity of the anonymous "Professor", with whom the sixth Lubavitcher Rebbe, Rabbi Yosef Yitzchok Schneersohn, wrote, that his father, Rabbi Sholom Dovber Schneersohn met, was not disclosed as Freud until 1998 in the publications of a "*Reshimah*" (No. 94) of Rabbi Menachem Mendel Schneerson and in the transcript of a Chassidic gathering from the year 1962, both published in 1998, cited above.

[16] As told at length by Rabbi J. Biderman, a Lubavitcher emissary in Vienna at: http://www.chabad.org/library/article_cdo/aid/1201321/jewish/The Rebbe-and-Viktor-Frankl.htm.

mental wellbeing of the human; to the reduction and sometimes the elimination of inner conflicts; and so also the "complaints" made about the [social and personal] context and so forth. This is notwithstanding the [Freudian psychoanalytical] approach [...] that belief and religious doctrine entail a submission [to norms and values], which bridle and crush the instincts and impulses, and therefore are not desirable in general; and particularly in the case of a personality which requires psychological treatment and the like. I have interested myself particularly in the writings of Dr Frankl (of Vienna) in this matter. To my astonishment, his approach has not been as widely disseminated and accepted as it should have been. And even though one could find a number of reasons for this phenomenon, that his approach has not been so widely accepted, including also that it is bound up with the living example of the treating therapist, nevertheless the question remains a question...[17]

In this letter, the Rabbi makes two points. First, he affirms, clearly from the standpoint of traditional religion, that mental health *is* served by the subordination of impulse and emotional conflict to spiritual values and moral imperatives. He rejects the idea that the submission of impulse to spiritual norms constitutes a somehow undesirable "crushing" of impulse, with claimed negative effects for mental health. Secondly, he clearly implies that it is essential that the therapist be a "living example" of a self-transcending personality. For, without this personal quality, the therapist cannot be a facilitator of self-transcendence in the patient, so important in Frankl's logotherapy. The first point concerns us here. The second has been discussed already in Chapter 1 of this Introduction.

The model of the integral personality in Frankl's logotherapy – highlighted and affirmed by the Seventh Lubavitcher Rabbi here – is a *hierarchical* one. It is expressed by a phrase in *The Unconditioned Human*, quoted earlier, that "the physical makes possible the mental realization of a spiritual demand". That is to say, (1) the soul (the "spiritual demand") instructs (2) the mind to realize its purpose in (3) the bodily or somatic-emotional realm. The control of emotion by intellect at the behest of the soul parallels a religious concept in the service of G-d, known in mystical teaching as *is'cafia* ("binding back") whereby impulse *is held in check and harnessed* by intellect in the service of the

---

[17] Cited above p. 3. Present writer's translation.

soul and its norms. Logotherapy is thus a psychological vehicle for *is'cafia*, the first level in the integration of the moral personality.

We spoke in Chapter 4 of the visit in the winter of 1902-1903 of Rabbi Sholom DovBer Schneersohn to Freud in Vienna. The aspect of the meeting, relevant to our discussion here, focussed on the Rabbi's low spirits as a result of his dissatisfaction with own his service of G-d in both the realms of heart and mind. Freud, understanding the Rabbi's greatness in *each* of these domains, produced, as we have noted, the diagnosis: "The heart desires more than the head can comprehend, and the head understands more than the heart can come to". This, he said, was "found only in profound and committed thinkers". We explained this in spiritual terms as expressing the independent heights reached by both understanding and feeling found in special individuals such as Rabbi Sholom DovBer.

The "discontent" arose from the fact emotion stood at a level of refinement where it could not be satisfied by intellect (and vice-versa). The question ostensibly is, how can emotion rise to a level of spiritual refinement in which it excels in certain respects that of the spiritually honed and refined intellect? It is not surprising that intellect can develop a high level of refinement in spiritual terms. It is normally the first recipient from the soul and, with its analytical and conceptual powers *as intellect*, is best equipped to receive them. As noted the common sequence is that feeling is subsequently trained by intellect. How could emotion become something higher than intellect could school it to be?

The answer to this has been given, above, by Chassidic thought itself. The rise to unique heights of the emotional self occurs through its own cleaving to the essence of the soul, such that it is transformed by the direct influence of the soul. Indeed, in mystical religious writing it is stated that the spiritual essence of the human being has a greater "proximity" to, and affinity with, the heart than it does with the mind, to the point that the essence of the soul is called the "will of the heart".[18]

---

[18] *Rei'usa d'liba*. It is interesting also to note that the "outer" legal framework of the Noahide laws – the rational, *intellectual* content of the "imitation of G-d" set out by the Maharal – applies to Frankl's logotherapy; whilst the more "inner", mystical teaching of the G-dly attributes *(s'firos)* embodied by the Noahide laws as intimated by the Maharal, applies to a revalued Freudian theory of the *instincts*, seen from the perspective of *emotion*. Just as the mystical, inner dimension stands higher than the rational, outer dimension, so does Freud's revalued theory address a higher or deeper level of the integrated moral personality, than does Frankl's. It may well be that Frankl intuited the superiority of refined emotion over intellect, when he wrote in *Der unbewusste G-tt*, "feeling can reach heights of subtlety, which are not matched by the heights of its intellect in its acuity"

This level of personality development known in religious tradition as *is'hapcha* – the *transformation* – of emotion stands higher than the constraint and control of emotion by intellect, *is'cafia*. "G-d desires the heart"[19] and there are two levels at which it can be His: *is'cafia* and *is'hapcha*. These two levels of integration of the human personality in the imitation of G-d provide a twin beacon for the psychologist For the way out of the "basement" or "mud-patch" of human personality can be found only by keeping in sight the heights of the human being, who in his or her soul was made as a moral being in the image of the G-d. With this model of the "well" person, psychology offers the means of ascent, beyond emergence from sickness, to ever greater levels of actualization of the Divine likeness within the person.

This sense of the well person is that of the spiritually well person – one whose mind and heart harmonizes with the soul. "Wellness", however, also of course has a pragmatic sense, that of one who – psychophysically – "functions" and "feels" well. Can these two senses of wellness be at odds with one another? Specifically, can a spiritually well person have residues of psychophysical – mental or somatic – illness? Conversely, can the person in whom the spirit is repressed and replaced with a pathological value set, yet psychophysically feel and function well?

Frankl found schizophrenic persons in whom a genuine spirituality broke through (as told in "The Science of the Soul"). And conversely, we find individuals with pathological value sets – such Nazi camp guards – who after a day of unspeakable cruelty, seem to have come home to a functional family and personal life. On the macroscale, moral societies have suffered and barbarous societies have prospered. So the answer seems to be "yes" – it is possible that spiritual wellness not coincide with practical and material wellness – but the "yes" is a highly qualified and limited one.

The reason for this, theologically speaking, is that human personality with its faculties was fashioned by the Creator as a "vessel" for – in correspondence to – the soul, as was society, for its harmonious and peaceful existence, created as a vessel for its "soul", the Noahide laws. It follows that a values template, at significant variance from the spiritual one, will ultimately (if not sooner) produce dysfunction in the vessel, whether in mental health or social functioning. Evidentially this is so, as confirmed by empirical psychological science,

---

(p. 49), the present writer's translation of "…*das Gefühl kann viel feinfühliger sein als der Verstand scharfsinnig*".

[19] *Zohar, parshas Ki Seitzei.*

noted in the Preface: overall mental health – practical, materially experienced wellbeing – correlates positively with spirituality.

The anomalies – the psychologically unwell but spiritual person and the psychologically "well" person with pathological beliefs – are also explained by the tradition from Sinai. The explanation is that, as a result of human sin, distortion has occurred in the nexus of nature – human, physical and societal – with the spiritual: the relationship of the spirit with nature, including psychophysical nature, can be impaired, indirect and delayed. The psychopath can flourish; the spiritual person can feel and function poorly. Barbarous societies can triumph and moral societies can function poorly, as noted. These anomalies, however, are relatively short-lived – they do not persist over the long term of human lives and societies – because they bespeak a dissonance between the ultimately irrepressible human spiritual essence and the material vessel created for it, which in the long term cannot properly work in contradiction and dissonance one with the other.[20]

In a redeemed world, with a repaired human and physical nature, the spontaneous correspondence (and "cooperation") of psychophysical nature and the human spirit will be visibly and wholly restored. The path towards this ideal both in the histories of individuals and societies is through progressive, partial refinements, met along the way with aberrations and regressions. With an as-yet not fully repaired human nature, one must therefore cope with a degree of "duality" between the wellness of the psychophysical organism, by its functional criteria, and the wellness of the spirit, expressed in its conscious sovereignty within the person. This coping advances through *is'cafia* – the piecemeal "checking" and redirecting of our psychophysical nature by the spirit – promoted by Frankl's logotherapy. The spirit contends with rampant impulse and wayward perception. It prevails over and despite them. Even when it does bring them into line with the soul, it has not fully eliminated their residual resistance, which is still heard, as Frankl puts it in "The Unconditioned Human", like the virtuoso playing on a badly tuned piano. But *is'cafia* is still an unquestionable human achievement, and there is great succour in it.

The next and higher step, intimated in the ideal of the reclaimed Freudian theory, is to transform the psychophysical elements, so that with their unique strengths they come to embrace and express the spirit. In the words of the

---

[20] Even though, for reasons known to their Creator, barbarous cultures may be sustained by an unnatural logic even up to the threshold of Redemption. See Rabbi Y. Y. Schneersohn, *"Reishis Goyim Amalek"*, *Sefer Maamorim 5680*.

tradition, *is'cafia* alters the attributes of our nature while *is'hapcha* alters the nature of our attributes. With the second step, where we succeed in achieving it, we advance, in some department of our personality, to a refined second nature: from a duality to a unity of the spirit and psychophysical nature. In the domain of this particular, accomplished refinement, that would be a full wellness.

That the religious tradition clarifies and brings together the psychological theories of Frankl and a reclaimed Freud, should not be seen as a mere "appropriation" of their thought for the spiritual "rediscovery of the human". For Frankl himself explicitly harked back to his physical and spiritual ancestor, the Maharal of Prague, as the source of his "dimensional ontology" of personality. And what Joseph Berke has called the "hidden Freud" (referring his "Chassidic roots") emerged from the recesses of Freud's Jewish soul in that remarkable encounter with Rabbi Sholom DovBer Schneersohn. Not only *can* the religious tradition claim both these great psychologists with major benefit. They *too* made themselves available in their engagements with the great Rabbis of the Chassidic tradition for integration with religious tradition.

TRANSLATIONS

TIME AND RESPONSIBILITY

A lecture held in Innsbruck
19 February 1947
by Dr Viktor E. Frankl

Translated by Shimon Cowen

Psychological malaise: existential, neurotic and psychotic[1]

Ladies and Gentlemen,

When asked whether the title of this lecture (originally: "The mentally ill person confronted with the question of the meaning of existence") was well chosen, I must say, no. If we further ask, how this doctor, that is, how *psychiatrists* in general have responded to the question of the meaning of existence, we have to say, not at all. In truth, it is much less the mentally ill person, than the doctor treating this person, who is faced the question of the meaning of existence. In general, they have simply dodged the question and swerved into psychologism.

Were I, for a better understanding of further considerations, quickly to define psychologism, I would offer the following provisional proposition. Psychologism tries to draw conclusions from the mental origins of an act as to the validity of its spiritual content. To use a somewhat gross example and conscious caricature (for the purposes of instruction) of the psychologistic procedure, this has the appearance of one who says: "The idea of G-d emerged from primitive man's primordial fear of the powers of nature. The present-day human – who has mastery over nature – no longer need have any fear. Consequently, there is no G-d."

This short-circuited reasoning from the developmental history [of psyche] – psychogenesis – onto its content, has, notwithstanding its invalidity and

---

[1] The captions have been inserted by the translator.

methodological coarseness, in fact flourished and namely within psychopathology. Indeed, one could say that psychologism has triumphed as psycho*patho*logism. In this particular manifestation of psychologism, by declaring the presence of pathological traits, there is simultaneously an immediate stipulation of the worthlessness [of the spiritual content of psyche].

Here is also revealed in the same moment the weakness which psychologism was always stuck with. For ultimately its principle consists in projecting phenomena *out of their own spiritual space down into the plane of the "psychological"*. Thereby, this approach loses not only an entire dimension, namely the spiritual dimension, but even more than this: the phenomena become in that moment ambiguous. Exactly the same happens to the psychologist as happens to someone who projects a solid cylindrical, conical or spherical object from a three-dimensional space into a (two-dimensional) plane. In this projection – in "outline" – all that ever results is a circle, and always the same circle, and from this projection it will never be clear with what one was dealing in the first place.

The same thing happens to the psychopathologist. For one, who projects every pattern – even spiritual patterns – onto the plane of the mentally ill, these patterns lose their clarity. As soon as one dispenses with reference to the particular spiritual content and has exclusively in view the mental event – the act but not the transcendent object intended in this act – so long as the observer proceeds in this way, he or she never knows whether something in a concrete instance represents a cultural achievement or merely a neurotic symptom.

Let us take an example. Assume we have to do with a despairing person – one who doubts meaning in life or the possibility of answering to life. This is a mentally ill person who throws up before us the "question of the meaning of existence." This is the actual state of affairs. So long as, and to the extent that, we persist with a purely psychological perspective, we shall never be able to resolve what this very state of affairs ultimately signifies. For, whether it accords with depression, the suicidal mood of a person with melancholic depression – that is to say, of a psychotic person – or the depression and corresponding mood of a neurotic (such as *Weltschmerz* in the case of a puberty neurosis); or finally simply the question of a – thoroughly healthy – person in each of these cases the identical fact is presented from the perspective of the solely-psychological: depression! This is so also when, in our case, a psychotically ill person *[Geisteskranke]* raises the question and in the second a neurotically ill *[seelisch Kranker]*, and in the final case of a human being – as human being (for only a human being as such is in general able to raise the question of his or her own existence; it is inconceivable that an animal could ask about its own meaning). However, upon the decision for which interpretation to opt – of what in the purely psychological plane is an ambiguous state of affairs – an entire further "therapeutic" procedure depends. For if it is a case of psychotic symptoms, then I will proceed simply as a psychiatrist: that is, I will not so much talk as act. I will under circumstances admit the depressed patient, because of the danger of suicide, in order to protect him for the duration of his illness. Finally, besides this, I will prescribe psychotropic medication to alleviate those feelings of anxiety, which arise from the organism, that is to say, are physiologically determined and form the basis of the whole weariness of life and despairing thoughts.

Indeed, I know that going into the ideas of a psychotically ill person is generally a wasted effort. As long as the patient is in the midst of a psychosis – such as melancholic depression – so is any beginning, the attempt at a correction of his or her ideas, totally hopeless. To illustrate this for you, I would like to speak of a relevant case, which stands out in my memory. It had to do with a woman who had already gone through many depressive phases, from each of which she had again emerged one hundred percent healthy. This woman now showed weariness of life and suicidal tendencies, just as she had in each of her previous episodes of illness, and justified this attitude with her (abnormal, though in terms of her disorder, explicable) interpretation that her life was completely meaningless and that because she was incurable further treatment was unnecessary. In response, now, to my objection that according to her case notes, she had believed this every single time and notwithstanding had been discharged fully recovered – just as in response to my indication of thirty-four records of similar illness, which lay on my desk and delivered the same message – she would always give me the same answer: "This time it is different. This time I will *not* become well again." Thus, one sees that one can never deal with a psychosis with *logical* arguments.

If, in the case of a psychosis, I am oriented solely as a psychiatrist – primarily towards the organic illness – so, in the case of a neurosis, which exhibits the identical features of depression, I again have to proceed differently. I will use psychotherapy (as in its original narrower meaning). That is, I will speak with the patient and in the course of conversations, set out to uncover the mental foundations of the mental disturbance, the mood disturbance (in contrast to its organic-physical basis in the case of a psychosis). I shall again in conversation and through conversation try to remove it. Accordingly, I shall function not as a psychiatrist but, more precisely, as a psychotherapist.

How is it now, from a medical point of view, with the question of the right and appropriate procedure in the case of neither a psychotic nor a neurotic foundation for the presenting depression, but when there sits before me a human being who poses to me, precisely as a human, this most human of all questions – the question of the meaning of his or her existence – struggling for an answer in order to find his or her way out of that depression: a depression, which at this stage is not at all the cause of thoughts of desperation, but rather their result? Now in such a situation, I will indeed also be obliged to engage myself also as a human being – that is to say, beyond anything medical in the traditional sense, beyond any psychopathological evaluation (as "sick" or "healthy", or as a symptom at all) – and enter an impartial discussion of all the arguments which the "patient" can bring forward. Certainly, I may no longer refer to this kind of procedure as psychotherapy, that is, as psychotherapy in the sense, which previously applied. Precisely because the procedure required here aims to overcome psycho(patho)logism, we wish to designate it as "logo-therapy". For this procedure enters the thought paths of the patient and does so with logical counterarguments. No longer does it proceed with medication – addressed to physical processes – and no longer with affective modifications of emotion – targeting the emotional dynamic of the patient – but rather with spiritual weapons, logotherapy seeks to gain influence in the spiritual struggle taking place within the patient.

The therapist's activation of the patient's responsibility

In saying here, that the physician in the pertinent case is *obligated* to answer a question not determined by illness, but rather a purely human question, there arises the dilemma, whether and to what extent, he or she – as *physician!* – is entitled to do so. For the danger is at once clear: the imposition of the personal world-view, that is, the private view of the physician onto the patient. For that, the patient certainly did not come to the professional. Yet, isn't it precisely the physician's task in this situation to bring the patient up to that point, where he or she comes to his or her own world-view and philosophy of life; where the patient takes responsibility for finding a new path of the spirit back to life? This indicates the solution of our problem, the way out of that dilemma for the physician, which appears to consist in the fact that on the one hand one has to intervene in the struggle of the spirit of the patient and, on the other hand, must refuse to do that. The way out of this dilemma is namely: the education of the patient to his or her own self-responsibility. Now we see also, how at this point, the essential difficulty of logotherapy pushes forward to a positive turn; or in other words, how an apparent weakness of this therapy becomes a strength.

For then, that outermost point, to which logotherapy may proceed, is seen not only as adequate to the therapeutic end-goal, but also as its pivot. For the human – and precisely the neurotic – has no greater need than to be as aware as possible of his or her own responsibility. That is why all psychotherapy, and especially logotherapy cannot sufficiently stress the responsibility of the person, and the person's freedom.

It is indeed so, that the human being everywhere – not only the neurotic – seems constantly engaged in trying to evade his or her responsibility, and instead of responding (whether to one's community or conscience, or one's G-d), by excusing oneself [of this task], one suppresses the consciousness of one's responsibility; one denies one's freedom and in playing off the counter-pole of freedom – fate – against freedom, thereby loses one's freedom in the gamble. To this end, a person makes various excuses for oneself. One conceals one's freedom behind so-called fate, whether from one's environment, one's inner world or also one's social world.

One hides oneself from freedom in relation to the *environment* by citing mitigating "circumstances". To the "environment" belong primarily all material factors – not only the coarsely material, but also "material" in the sense in which the materialist conception of history speaks; that is, in the sense of economic relationships. That, and the extent to which, a human being possesses at least a certain scope of freedom vis-à-vis ostensible fate, is not something which we want now to investigate further. It should be sufficient to note that such a space of freedom, when not so explicitly acknowledged, was also tacitly assumed by that same properly understood socialism.

In regard to the *inner world*, now, in terms of the ostensibly fateful aspects of which the human being frequently excuses him- or herself: these are not circumstances, but rather certain mental states or tendencies, also biologically based predispositions, to which the human and specifically, the mentally ill, tend to return. Primarily, here is that which Freudian psychoanalysis called the "Id" which is experienced as fateful, particularly by the neurotic. It is this "Id" which serves as a pretext, when the surrender of freedom is at issue. In view of what was mentioned at the outset – that the neurotic human particularly needs the awakening of the consciousness of responsibility – it is now clear that the psychoanalysis possibly plays into the hands of the neurotic tendency of self-excuse.

We do not hesitate to state that Freud's psychoanalysis is indeed the classical method of psychotherapy. As such, it can today be observed as "historical" – "historical" with the double, sentimental loading, which attaches to this word. Intellectually-historically seen, this movement was necessary. However, impartially considered, it has today become impossible and untenable. This is possibly so also of the history of the Enlightenment: the Enlightenment was highly necessary in its time and had its mission in its time. This mission, however, has long since been fulfilled, has outlived itself and is outdated. However, should it surprise us if the same has happened to psychoanalysis within the historical development of psychotherapeutic methods – is not psychoanalysis perhaps itself best understood as a kind of Enlightenment of the "inner" self?

We have already intimated that a certain tendency is characteristic of the neurotic: to escape the consciousness of his or her self-responsibility and freedom in that he or she finds refuge in purportedly or ostensibly fated circumstances and conditions. It has to do, one could say, with the sense of neurotic fatalism. This fatalism expresses itself primarily in *that the neurotic puts up with everything that presents itself to him, in his mental state.* Let us ask ourselves, however, whether the dispositions – the diverse psychological and biological factors, which a person encounters in him- or herself – are really there in order to be put up with? Let us then ask ourselves whether also freedom, which constitutes the deepest basis of human existence, has at least some small say? Now it is indeed so that [personal] dispositions obtain. That means, however, that they are ready and available – but to whom? Precisely our freedom! Human freedom rests on an ability to exercise control, that is, it has the power of decision. The so-called *dispositions* of the human are *by no means* that which from the outset could determine one's *(psychological and biological) destiny.* Rather they have a thoroughly *positive aspect*, and this becomes visible only, where we grasp them as being at the *"disposition of"* – freedom.

The meaning of freedom

For its part, however, this freedom has a double aspect, negative and positive. Negatively, it is "free from" and positively, it is "free to." *It is freedom from "being so" [Sosein] and freedom to "existence" [Dasein].* Ultimately, the existence of the person consists in being responsible. Consequently the essential freedom of the person – as distinct from the fated being-so, vis-à-vis the inner dispositions – is a *possession of control over.* Exactly so, it signifies from a higher perspective – from the positive side – *having responsibility*.

We have already heard that, and to what extent, the accentuation on being-responsible is necessary for the neurotic existential modality. We now need to ask, whether and how this is possible.

This can be possible via a method (of psychological diagnosis as well as a psychotherapeutic treatment) which allows *the autonomy of the spiritual existence* to take the place of the *automatism of the psychological "apparatus"*, which is the way psychoanalysis grasps human existence. We call this approach existential analysis. In the same moment we are aware of that positive twist of logotherapy, of which we spoke and said that it makes an apparent weakness into a strength: the *twist*, inasmuch as it proceeds around *the pivot of* the central *responsibility* of the person, at once signifies *logotherapy suddenly changing into existential analysis*. For what else is existential analysis other than an analysis of human existence in relation to the person's essential being-responsible?

Thereby is already manifest the significance of existential analysis in connection with today's theme, the question of the meaning of existence. For, in fact, existential analysis, as an interpretation of the human being – as interpretation of human existence – is the attempt at an answer to the question of the meaning of this being. To indicate, in a few words, how it strives towards this goal, let us mark the most important stations along this way. First, existential analysis gives the question of the meaning of life a dialectical twist. It explains that it is not the person who here needs to raise a question, but rather, paradoxically, it is life itself which asks the person. Accordingly, it becomes clear that we can only answer the question life poses to us when we answer our life. The answer, which we have to give, is thereby an active one. More than this, it can only be a concrete one. It can only result in answering our particular life, in answering our being there [*Dasein*] in the here and now. This answerability to existence – in its utmost concreteness and specificity to my particular person as well as to the particular situation – constitutes the sought meaning of existence: being-responsible is the meaning of human existence!

The past, the present and the future

Now, however, an important question arises. We have spoken all along of being and apparently forgot about becoming: coming-to-be and passing-away. We forgot that so little of that which is, *remains* – stays – in our existence. We forgot the patent transitoriness of all being. How, therefore, we now have to ask ourselves, can *responsibility* – the fundamental characteristic of our existence – be maintained, in view of the transitoriness of all being?

When we fully take in, in its complete depth, the impression, which the transitoriness of all being makes upon us, we come to that point, at which we can only say: the future does not (yet) *exist* and the past does not exist (any more). What *is* real, is only the present. Alternatively, we could also say: the future is *nothingness* and the past is similarly *nothingness*. Accordingly, the human being is poised as an entity, which comes from nothingness – is born from nothingness, "thrown" into being, and threatened by nothingness. In this respect, the human is a truly exalted being, a "from" and a "to": from nothingness to nothingness! This would be nothing more than a word-play, had not contemporary philosophy itself seriously formulated it so. It is thus presented as the nobility of the human and his or her greatness – and is indeed called a "tragic heroism", that the human emerges from nothingness and heads into nothingness and *nevertheless* says "yes" to his or her own existence.

What we have before us, as you will have noticed, is the point of departure of existential philosophy [as distinct from existential analysis]. We can grasp its fundamental thesis – of the authentic reality and the sole significance of the present – as the counter-pole to the outlook of quietism. The latter, connecting with Plato and Augustine, sees, instead of the present, eternity as the ultimate reality: indeed an "eternity" in the sense of a simultaneous four-dimensional reality – a *nunc stans*, of an inflexible, fixed reality – foreseen and predetermined forever. Here is retracted not only the reality of the future and the past, but the reality of time itself. In this conception, time is rather a mere illusion. Coming-to-be and passing-away, the division into future, present and past is only an illusion of consciousness. This consciousness, moreover, glances, so to speak, like a searchlight over intrinsically simultaneous being, giving the appearance of sequence, a coming and going, to that, which in reality, all *remains* together.

Now, clearly this quietism has the immediate consequence of a fatalism. A person will come from it to believe, one simply has to fold one's arms, since everything already "is" regardless. This *fatalism*, however, which results in the quietist perspective of *eternal being*, finds its counterpart in the *pessimism*, which necessarily results from the view, held by *existential philosophy*, of the process of *constant* becoming, of the impermanence of being, of becoming and passing away.

If you want to understand the position of existential *analysis* vis-à-vis [and in opposition to] existential *philosophy*, on the one hand, and quietism, on the other, it would be desirable for me to clarify the two different and opposed concepts, of which we have just spoken, by means of an analogy. Consider, as a symbolic representation of time, an hourglass. In the upper part we have the future before us, that which is yet to come: sand which is yet to flow through the narrow section of the hourglass. In the lower part is the past, what has already been, the sand that has already passed through this narrow section. This narrow passage itself, however, represents the present. What, now, does existential philosophy do? It sees only this narrow section of the hourglass – the bottleneck of the present – and denies the upper and lower receptacles, the future and the past. Quietism, on the other hand, whilst it sees the hourglass in its totality, the sand itself is perceived as a rigid mass, which also in reality does not "flow". Much rather, in the quietist perspective, it is consciousness which slides through the "bottleneck of consciousness"(!) over the immobile, four-dimensional, simultaneous or timeless-eternal reality. In this perspective, the sand does not slip through the narrow pass, but rather the narrowness [of consciousness] through the sand.

Existential *analysis* maintains now that the truth is, in fact, approximately in the middle. It says, namely, the future is truly nothing; but the past is the authentic truth! How does existential analysis come to this concept? This can be further explained through the analogy of the hourglass.

The analogy of the hourglass, like every analogy, is somewhat deficient. Yet precisely through it, one can see the deepest significance of time. Now, it is part of the use of an hourglass, that we can turn it upside down as soon as the upper receptacle in empty. Time, however – and this pertains to its essence – cannot be turned around; it is irreversible! More than this, however: when we shake and joggle the hourglass, we thoroughly mix up the sand grains amongst each other. With time, it is different, at least partly. The future is indeed mobile or better put, it is at our disposition. We have power over it: we can make it different or ourselves become different. But the past is fixed! In the lower receptacle of the hourglass, "time" – to return to the analogy – the sand, which has already passed through the narrow pass, the "present," is fixed. It is thus as though there were in this part of the receptacle something like a setting-agent, or better put, a preservative. For in fact, in the past, everything which has passed is *aufgehoben* in the twofold Hegelian sense of this word. Not only is it "liquidated", but it is also now in safekeeping – preserved. Hence, it is not as though the sand in the lower receptacle were "dissolved" through some kind of solution.

The "optimism of the past" and "activism of the future"

Existential analysis poses now, in the light of the actual transitoriness of all being, the following claim. Truly *transitory* are only the *possibilities*, the chances of the actualization of values, the opportunities, which we have. These are to create or to experience – or to suffer (that is, proper suffering, honest suffering of that which is truly unalterable, which is authentically fated). Once we have *actualized* these possibilities[2], they are no longer "transitory", rather they are past, they exist as something past, which means that, in their past-ness, they continue to exist! For precisely in their past-ness, they are indeed preserved and nothing more can touch them. Nothing can remove from the world what has once happened, what has passed. It exists, as past, *once and for all*, and "for all eternity."[3]

We now see how existential analysis counterposes an optimism of the past to the pessimism of the purely present aspect of existential philosophy. I once sought to clarify the question of how the optimist of the past relates to the pessimist with the following analogy. The pessimist can be compared to a

---

[2] Corresponding to this threefold opportunity of actualizing values, we speak of creative, experiential and attitudinal values [see below pp. 105-6].

[3] What is finished is conclusively finished, but it is also current in its concludedness. In having come to an end, it remains current and to that extent it remains in existence. In view of the irreversibility of the actualized, we must now ask ourselves, how is it with such matters as regret and atonement? Do they contradict that irreversibility? No – because regret and atonement are themselves also actualizations. Moreover, the overcoming of fate, as this results through the realization of attitudinal values, that is, the redemption of past history, has in the meantime itself become history, namely something accomplished [through this attitude]. In other words, regret is as indelible as guilt! Also, once in a deed (truly, we should say, a misdeed) a creative value has been *actualized*, through regret *an attitudinal value* can also further be realized. That, ultimately, realized attitudinal values can – in the right relationship towards the past for which one is to blame, as itself a fated given – deliver the platform for the realization of *newer creative values* is evident. Banally put, from the mistakes of the past, we learn for the future, or to state it less trivially, and to speak with Schopenhauer, no money is better invested than that of which we allowed ourselves to be cheated: for that we receive an immediate wisdom in exchange. It is the *attitudinal values,* however, which are the only ones that can be realized literally to the last moment. For literally until the last moment it is possible for a person to take up an attitude to a fated circumstance or to change one's attitude to *any* fated circumstance, and thereby also to one's life's totality, now fated because it is now finished. Thus and only so, can it also be understood that people have come to the comprehension that an entire life can also be retrospectively atoned for, sanctified and made meaningful – through a single great regret in a solitary small moment, even "in the last moment".

person who stands before a wall calendar and sadly observes how the calendar becomes ever thinner, as he tears off a page every day. The optimist, on the other hand, is like one who very carefully lays the calendar page, which he has once removed, neatly upon the other removed pages, noting on its reverse side what he did or experienced that day; and not without pride looks back at the whole of what has been undertaken in these pages, all that that his been lived and consolidated in this life of his.

Think again what such a standpoint in relation to past-ness – whereby we from now on always accentuate the "being" [the present-ness of the past] – can signify practically in the life of a person. Imagine the despair of a war widow, who viewed her future life as meaningless for the reason that she lost her husband and had perhaps experienced only one year of the happiness of marriage. What must it mean to her to hear know that *she has after all this one year of pure happiness "behind her", that she has "rescued it" into the [ever present] being of the past, where it is secured "for all time"; and that nothing and no one can ever take away the fact of having had this experience?*

One can ask, who, after the death of this woman will preserve "in life" the memory of her husband and her happiness? To that the following can be said: whether she or anyone recollecting, thinks back to it, or not, is immaterial; just as it is immaterial whether we think or look on at something which presently remains beside us. It endures independently of our awareness and the devotion of our awareness to it. Thus, everything remains, not only independently of our subjective turning towards it, but also, so independently continues to remain. It is true that "we take nothing with us into the grave". But is not the totality of life, which we have lived, and in dying, have lived to its completion, something which remains outside any grave and moreover, outside of it also remains? This is not something remaining, despite transitoriness, but is preserved precisely in its being-past[4].

Death as the summons and achievement of self

Now, everything passes. No one should surrender to the illusion that a bodily being, such as the physical child, which we have set in the world, is any less

---

[4] This remaining preserved in its being-past is not interrupted, when that which is a past event is lost from consciousness. What has gone from consciousness cannot be done away with from the world. Rather it is, and remains something "created into the world". Indeed, even when it never entered any consciousness, it has come into the world! To identify continuing-to-be, in the past, with "being remembered" would be an entirely subjectivist or psychologistic reinterpretation of our conception of the character of being of that which is, in being past.

transitory than say the great thought or the great love from which this child may have arisen. All this is equally transitory. [As the verse states (Psalms 90:10)] "A person's life lasts seventy years, and at a height, eighty, and if it was goodly, then it was with trouble and work…" In time, the great thought lasts perhaps seven seconds; and if it was good, it contained truth. But transitory it is, the great thought, just as much as, and no more so, than the young child or the great love. *Everything* is transitory.

But everything is also eternal! And not only that, but it becomes eternal by itself. That is why we do not have to worry that "we" make it eternal. For as soon as we have effected it – as soon as it has been effected through our life – it automatically makes itself eternal. We therefore do not have to worry *that* something should last forever: but all the more are we responsible for *what* has all been made eternal, in that it has been effected by us.

Everything is recorded in the "logbook" of the world – our entire life and all we have created, our love and suffering. It is "recorded" in this log and "taken up": it remains preserved within them. It is not the way a great existentialist philosopher sees it – that the world, so to speak, is a manuscript, which, moreover, is written in a "code-language". *No, the world is not a manuscript, which has to be deciphered (and cannot be deciphered) – the world is much rather a record, which we have to dictate!*

This record, moreover, has a dramatic character. Martin Buber[5] indeed has taught us that the life of spirit is not a monologue, but a dialogue. Have we not found out the same: that it is *life*, which constantly asks *us* questions? Don't we finally understand *why* the record of the world is dramatic? – Because the record has to do with our life and *our life is ultimately an interrogation. Life constantly asks us questions. Constantly we answer life; truly, life is question and answer; seriously.*

The logbook of the world cannot be lost. That is our comfort and our hope. It is not, however, only unlosable but also non-correctable[6]. That is a warning

---

[5] It should be noted, however, that Buber's philosophy at the same time falls short of Frankl's own criterion of the connection of moral responsibility to commitment to a higher law, which in Buber's case was the failure to connect to the traditional law of Judaism. See below p. 114, "Responsibility" is thus even more so a binding-back together of freedom, a recoupling with a (higher) order in the sense of law. Binding-back together, in this sense, is – no less and no more – the literal translation [of the word] re-ligio". In this sense, the *existentialist* element in Buber's thought prevails – Transl.

[6] See, however, footnote 3, where Frankl speaks of regret and atonement as actualizations – Transl.

and a reminder to us. For when we said that nothing past can be done away with from the world, isn't that also a reminder not to bring it into the world? It will now be evident that we have to oppose to the pessimism (of the present) in the existentialist philosophy not only an *optimism of the past*; simultaneously we have to counterpose to a quietest fatalism an *activism of the future*. For precisely in view of the "eternal" preservation of being in its being-past, it will be all important *what* we – in the present, in the moment – *"create into"* *this being-past*.

But what actually is this "creating into being", into the past? It is ultimately creation out of a void – out of the void of the future!

Now, we can also understand why all being is so transitory, why everything is fugitive. Everything is so fugitive because it is in flight! In flight from the void of the future into the being of the past. As though in horror of a vacuum, in terror of the void, everything fears the void of the future and plunges into the past and its being. Standing before the bottleneck of the present, it swells and surges and there *"everything awaits redemption"*…for the redemption which will fall to his or her lot, *in that it – as event – in coming to pass, enters the being of the past; or, as our experience and our decision – is allowed by us into eternity.*

The bottleneck of the present, this narrow place, which, from the void of the future, leads over into the (eternal) being of the past, is now – as border-zone between void and being – at once the border-zone of eternity. From this it follows no less that eternity, as bordered, is actually a *finite* eternity. It only ever extends up to the present – up to that present, where *we decide* what will be admitted into eternity. Thus, this border-zone of eternity, the border-zone between the void of the future and the being of the past is altogether *that place where, in every moment, the decision is made, what, as effected by us, will by itself become eternal.*

We now see something further. When, in general, one speaks of winning time, one thinks of a gaining of time through postponement into the future. We know, however, that we *"gain time"* – we gain "within" time, or we gain time "for ourselves" – *in that, instead of deferring something into the future, we, to the contrary, rescue it into the past.*

What happens when the hourglass – which has so long served us as an analogy – runs out? What happens when time has run out and therefore existence has *flowed out to finality*? This is the case in death.

In death, all is immobile; nothing is at one's disposition. The human being no longer has anything for his or her use – no *body* and no *mind* can be utilized.

One has arrived at the total loss of the psychophysical "I". All that remains is the *self*, the *spiritual* self. After death the person has no longer any "I". One "has" nothing more; one "is" now only: one's very self.

If one wants to claim that in death, a person sees – like a falling mountain climber – his whole life like a film sequence played over again before him at incredible speed, this could now be said: in death, the person becomes the *film itself*. He *is* now his life, his lived life. He *is* his own history, both what happened to him and what he effected. So is he also – according to what he did – his own Heaven and his own Hell.

But now we come to the paradox that a person's *own past* is the *real future*, which he or she has to face[7]. In death the person indeed has no life; but for that reason is his or her life. The fact that it is the past life, which he or she from now on "is", should no longer trouble us – for don't we know that having-been is overall the securest form of being?

This having-been is properly a having-been in the perfect tense – by no means in the imperfect, continuous tense! For life is now completed – as something completed, it indeed now "is". In the course of time, in the course of life – just as the grains of sand run through the narrow pass of the hourglass – ever new individual accomplishments enter the past. Now, after death, the entire life, the life-totality enters into being-past, as something perfectly accomplished!

This leads us, however, to a second paradox and a two-sided one at that. When we said that we create something into the world, in that we work it into the being of the past, then it is first, the person who works himself into the world, *who sets "himself" into the world*. Secondly, he is not set into the world with his birth, but rather he first sets himself into the world in *death*.

If, however, we remember that it is the self which one sets into the world in death (itself), then this paradox will no longer astonish us. For the self really "is" not; it is yet to "become". It can only "be" as *something which has become*; more precisely as something which has become *completely*. And complete it is, only in the moment of death.

To be sure, death is repeatedly misunderstood by the everyday person. When the alarm clock rings and startles us out of a dream, then, still caught in dream, we experience the awakening stimulus as a fearful invasion of the dream-world. We do not know that the alarm is waking us to an authentic being, to the daily world. Doesn't the same happen to a dying person? Are

---

[7] The living person has past and future. The dying person has no further future, only past. The dead person *is* his past.

we mortals not terrified by death? Do we not also misunderstand that, and to what extent, it awakes us to a more authentic, a more real reality of our self?

As for the tender hand, which wakes us out of sleep, however tender its movement may be – we still do not experience its full tenderness. No, we experience it as a fearful invasion of our dream reality, as soon as it tries to scare away our sleep. Similarly, we experience death, which takes our life away from us, as something fearful which happens to us and we have hardly any intimation of how well its intention is for us…

Time and circumstance as the context of responsibility

Earlier we said that death is misunderstood by the everyday person. That says too little: *time* is misunderstood! For what is the relationship of the average person to "time"? *He sees only the stubble field of transitoriness – but he does not see the full granary of the past.* He wants time to stand still, so that all will not be transient. But in this he is like a person who wants a reaping and threshing machine to stand still and work where it is, not as it travels. For, while the machine rolls over the field, he sees with a shudder the ever increasing stubble field, *but not the simultaneously growing mass of kernels inside the machine.* Thus, a person tends to see in past things only that they are no more there, *but he does not see, into what storage containers they have come.* He then says, they are *gone*, because things are transitory. But he should say, in their past-ness, they *are*, for once effected, they are forever eternalized.

Here we pause and recollect what has been laid out. Responsibility, as the most fundamental basis of human existence, is by no means nullified in its ultimate significance by the transitoriness of all being. To the contrary, the *being-responsible* of the human being, as the meaning of his or her existence, is in fact *founded* in *transitoriness.* As we have seen, it is founded precisely in the "activism of the future", which arose from the "optimism of the past": out of the knowledge of the *being* of that which is past.

Having at the outset submitted *psychologism* and *biologism*, as deniers of human freedom, to a critical light and having thereby seen how little justified fatalism, and especially neurotic fatalism, is, we need now to turn to a no less necessary critique of *sociologism*. Like psychologism and biologism, it wants to eclipse the freedom and the being-responsible of the human. Sociologism (and naturally not sociology as such) allows the human, instead of answering for, to excuse, him or herself. This time the excuse is not with reference to the *environment* or the *inner world* – to material circumstances or psychophysical conditions – but rather with regard to the *social world*, the collectivity. Here one speaks, not as in psychologism, of the "Id", in Freud's sense, but rather of the "One" or the "They" *[das "Man"]* in the sense of Heidegger. Again, one plays off apparent fate – which one ostensibly has to suffer as the supposed mere object of sociological laws and determinations – against one's *a priori* freedom. But there is no collective excuse! A person always has a certain scope of freedom even in the face of the bonds and influences of the collectivity. *One can* allow oneself to be influenced by them, but by no means does one *have to.* One can always do otherwise. When one believes, or pretends, not to be able, when one apparently has no more freedom, then one has – in fact voluntarily – renounced one's freedom.

It is true: if we want to dispute collective excuse, we must take the further step of concluding that collective *guilt* cannot be simply ascribed.

Opening the human subject

At the beginning of our investigation, we took pains to establish that existential analysis, as the analysis of human existence in terms of responsibility, is *necessary*, and not least as a psychotherapeutic method, and indeed in contradistinction to psychoanalysis. Further, we have undertaken to establish that existential analysis is also *possible.* That is, possible as the making conscious of our possession of responsibility – the responsibility and freedom of the human also in the face of those psychological, biological and sociological conditions, which confront one primarily as fated. In relation to this question of the possibility of an existential analysis, there arises a final question. Is existence, we now ask, in general capable of analysis?

We are again compelled to clarify this matter by means of an analogy, which alone can and should provide the answer. It is known that the point in the centre of the retina, where optical impressions are most *clearly* received – that point which, for this reason, is explicitly called the "point of clearest vision" – is by no means identical with the point which sees *most brightly!* Anyone can readily observe that in twilight or darkness one best perceives contrast; and that one best views the last visible contours of objects, when looking at them not directly but askew. The same happens with the researcher, who tries to get in view *the being of the human person, the modality of human-being – that which we call "existence". As soon and as long as one makes the authentic being of the human into an object in the sense of natural science, it will not at all disclose itself to one.* All one will see is the "being-so" [the outer properties] which inhere *in* the person, the being-so, which a person *has,* but one will never glimpse the being – that existence which the person (and only he or she), as such *"is".*

Only when we view human existence *not from the central vantage point of the "exact" natural sciences* [...], *will there come into view*, not only the being-so of the person, but also human existence, that is, *the essence of the human being.*

A final question. Granted that in this sense, existential analysis is not only *necessary* but *possible*, is the person of today, in particular, today's doctor also *capable* of this view? Let us not forget the developmental sequence, marked by the following stages: the birth of naturalism and, as an application of the natural sciences, technologism, at the beginning of modernity [followed by] the maturation of naturalism and the technologism in the nineteenth century. Both had necessarily to rub off on medicine and medical treatment. Thus, it happened that medicine – still at the beginning of modernity (one thinks simply of Paracelsus) through and through an *art* of healing – was degraded in the nineteenth century to a *science* of healing and in our century has fully sunk to a mere technics of healing. It is precisely medicine in which the centuries-old naturalism and technologism have most amalgamated, merging into what is indeed called biotechnology.

That all the empiricism, with which the doctor now approaches the object – namely, the human subject – has brought with it a total objectification of the person, is self-evident. This is clearest in a scientific phenomenon such as behaviouralism. It has entirely brought about that the human person – who in essence is constituted through free (spiritual) self-conduct in relation to a (physical or mental) empirical reality – is itself made into a mere empirical fact.

However, the human person has its weapons and moves to protect itself against the attempt at being made completely banal, reified and objectified – just as against the devaluation, which it thereby experiences – the degradation of the human. This weapon is shame. With this the person protects him- or herself against the full surrender and deliverance of his or her innermost being to the objectifying, natural-scientific view. No one should believe that this innermost, intimate aspect – which the person protects against the cold, sober eye – has to do with "intimacies" in the traditional *sexual* sense, which especially need to avoid the clutches of psychoanalysis. Oh no. Also, the intimate *religious* life resists gratuitous exposure and exhibition. I know a female patient, who in psychotherapy, without the least inhibition, spoke in detail about every sexual adventure, whilst she had the greatest inhibitions in – and I, as professional, the greatest difficulties to bring her to – speaking about her innermost religious experience.

The doctor may never forget what Nietzsche said: "The most human is to spare someone shame". At most only the doctor of the body – that is the doctor in the narrowest sense – can afford to ignore that. The surgeon can afford to make the person into a pure object – indeed, he must do it. For he knows all too well, in surgical interventions, how disturbing it is, when he perceives the patient as human – especially when he hears the patient cry.

We said that the surgeon can allow himself to make the patient totally into an object – the object of an operation. He screens out the reality of the person as a subject, as a person. This screening out is achieved practically. Whatever does not belong to the "field of operation", the field of action, of the patient, is literally "covered up" (namely, with sterile surgical drapes).

Existential analysis, however, when *it* makes the person the "object" of a particular psychotherapy, may by no means ignore the subject-character of the person. To the contrary, it is "co-operation" *with* the subject! It must *grasp* the person – by definition – *as an "existential" being* and, with this subject-character, leave him his freedom and responsibility. More than this, it must first *provide* him with his freedom and responsibility. For then and only then, is it able to appeal to his responsibility. That is what it is there for!

The doctor must ever pull him- or herself back into that human perspective, from which he or she sees the human in the object: the human being as human being. To be able to do this, however, he or she will then need to ask, "What would I do in the situation of this person?" Through this, one has already transposed oneself into the existence of the other. This transposition leads one, certainly beyond merely medical – such as the surgical – goal-determination. It signifies the turning from purely medical care to pastoral care carried out by the physician. This begins, however, precisely where the surgical action ceases. When the surgeon takes off his operating gloves – for example, after having established the inoperability of a tumour in the course of an exploratory laparotomy, or where he has performed an operation – and now, as it were, has to fold his arms: there begins the issue of medical-spiritual care – what will, what should, the patient do? What attitude should he or she take to the fact of being incurable or becoming an invalid? In this sense, existential analysis is less therapy of the organism than a theory relating to the person – to that spiritual dimension, which itself can never (not even in the so-called mentally ill) become sick, but which much rather takes up an attitude towards any illness, physical or mental.

Attitudinal, experiential and creative values

Here, however, one rule applies: first learn, then teach. For how often do we doctors observe – in regard to the achievements of our patients, in the accomplishment of a suffering individual in the face of the hardest fated difficulties – that it would be much more often appropriate for us to be filled with a sense of respect rather than the will to instruct!

What then could we learn from some of our patients? It has to do with the realization of what I have described as attitudinal values: those values, namely, which are realized in that we somehow take up an attitude to a fated circumstance; those values, which come into play as *the way* one relates to a fated state of affairs, *the way* one takes this circumstance upon oneself as one's burden, *the way* one suffers.

It is clear from the outset, that an attitudinal value in this sense can only be realized when the circumstance to which the person takes up an attitude is truly fated; that is, that it is truly unalterable. For it would be internally contradictory for a person to surrender him- or herself to suffering, endurance or tolerance of something which did not constitute a *necessary* suffering and nevertheless see in it a valuable achievement. (This would be the case, were I, for example, to refuse the operation on a thoroughly operable tumour – in order to shoulder my "burden", or alternatively, were I to refuse an achievable struggle for the social betterment of my person or my social class, on the grounds that misery refines one.)

Certainly, the actualization of attitudinal values contains the dimension of freedom, a voluntaristic dimension, but that we should voluntarily suffer and thereby achieve something of value, should not be so misunderstood as to apply to the case that we *wantonly* bring suffering upon ourselves, an avoidable suffering, for which we are therefore to blame. This problem is certainly related to the [...] problem of martyrdom. Martyrdom can be religiously acknowledged as such, when it is undertaken freely, but not wantonly.

Responsibility, so we have heard, is held for the realization of the passing opportunities for an actualization of values, and thereby to create something (valuable) into the being of the past, that is, into authentic being. We have also already indicated that this actualization can be achieved equally through a suitable activity, as well as through an experiencing or a suffering (naturally, a right suffering of an authentically fated circumstance). We have also pointed to the fact that besides attitudinal values, of which we have previously spoken, creative as well as experiential values are also possible [...]

From the variety of the three characterized categories of value, and the constant succession of opportunities for the respective actualization of each of them in life, it follows no *less* that *life – as something answered* constantly and under all circumstances – signifies for us *a task in every situation.* Therewith, it is further indicated that our existence – *all of our existence, and in every single moment of it, has an ever different, ever changing, but always some kind of meaning.* Indeed from this follows even further, that the greater the difficulties may be, these come upon us only to increase the task-character of our existence, and thereby the meaning of life.

The reality of religious experience

Now, as is ever evident, there are people, who do not experience their life as a task, but as a mission: as a mission, given by G-d. In other words, they experience the mission-Giver also. These are religious people. Without doubt it is also the concern of existential analysis to address the experience of these people, the religious modality of experience. We come now to a chapter, which could be called the existential analysis of the *homo religiosus.*

First of all, such an existential analysis would have to establish that the One experienced as having furnished the religious person with his or her life mission is by no means an authority of thing-like character but much rather is unambiguously experienced as personal – as a personal G-d. You will surely not require that existential analysis – even of the religious experiential modality – supply proofs of the existence of G-d. Quite apart from the fact that this is not the business of an existential analysis as such, my personal view – or let us better say, my personal feeling – is that all proof of the existence of G-d is perhaps ultimately blasphemous. For, let us ask: what can one prove, what is provable? Only ontic – that is to say, innerworldly – things, things somehow *within* nature. Thus, one can prove that there was some antediluvian animal: from fossilized footprints one can deduce a primordial existence. *But G-d is no fossil!* One cannot reason to Him as to ontic entities – not as to a natural entity, an entity *within* nature. No ontic path, at all events, leads to a being of the existential category which relates to G-d, but rather only an ontological [a *meta*physical path]. I cross over to Him (as such, that is not as any being within the world which I as a being face), when I understand myself, my entire being as something borne, as borne by an absolute foundation. (To understand my existence as one made [in the sense of human or natural fashioning], would not constitute an authentic ontological self-conception, since it would transfer a category – namely, causality – which is valid only within the natural realm, into the supernatural, the ontological realm). Only reason can perform logical inference. Reason, however, must fail not only in the face of that which is out of the world [- metaphysical –] but also in relation to the microphysical. It is well known that the categories with which we operate in everyday life, leave us in the lurch, when it comes to the atomic, nuclear physical realm. Reason functions, so to speak, only in the middle realm! Both what is *above* and beyond in the metaphysical realm, as well as what is below and beyond, in the microphysical realm, can be expressed through the intermediate means of our reason only in quotation marks! Not only are all our *metaphysical* interpretations no more than intimations; so also the ultimate basic concepts of *physics* are highly determined in their expression by the vocabulary of our ordinary language usage. One may want to criticize religion, in that its concept of G-d is *all too anthropomorphic*, and thereby indicate that no anthropopathic [human-emotive] characteristics can be claimed in relation to G-d – such as that He loves and is angry and avenges. But if such is argued against religion, then one is equally justified in objecting that concepts such as "force and matter" are no less anthropomorphic, and nevertheless, they persist in the language of physics – just like statements about the intended G-d of prayer. Of course, they are conditioned, metaphorical and analogical, *but still somehow valid*. If these statements – equally in the metaphysical as in the microphysical realm – are all too human and *all too concrete*, then other statements, in that realm beyond the middle-realm of our reasoning, are again *too abstract*. Criticism is made of this also. But here, too, it is evident that the abstract, the "unempirical" claims about G-d (in contradistinction to the intended G-d of prayer) – such un-empirical expressions, as of an "Absolute", and "*Ens realissimum, a se*" etc. – are no more non-empirical and abstract than those mathematical formulae, to which our modern physicists are forced to have recourse as ultimate conceptual principles.

It is thus unjustified to demand *logical proofs* for the existence of G-d specifically if these are required from the standpoint of existential analysis – an existential analysis of the *homo religiosus*. Admittedly, it is quite different in regard to the possibility of what one could call a *phenomenological demonstration*. (In this connection, we disregard a further possibility, namely that of referring – [that is,] the possibility of our being referred – out of immanent nature into the transcendent, by suchlike as conscience; imagining this as a kind of moral instinct which [could] point out of the ontic world into ontological [metaphysical] being. [In fact] we can never advance [from the one to the other] by *logical reasoning*.) How [then] could we now imagine such a phenomenological demonstration?

The classical example for the way such a procedure would have to follow, is perhaps the famous statement of Pascal, "I would not have sought YOU, had I not already found YOU." *The metaphysical reality is displayed as a transcendent one out of the intentionality of the act which intends it.* Recourse is made to the "metaphysical need" [the need which relates to, and is requited by, the metaphysical]. I do not believe at all that it is here necessary to grasp this metaphysical need of the human as an essentially theoretical one. It is perfectly conceivable that we would not be able to find the way beyond immanence into transcendence from a theoretical need, let alone out of an emotional one. It is thoroughly conceivable in the following way – not by "deducing" or even by "demonstrating or proving" – but by bringing to manifestation:

That which is to be loved precedes loving. Our love finds no satisfaction in anything which is found within the world. That in which our love *could* find satisfaction – this we call G-d; and insofar *is* G-d. Or: that which is to be revered precedes reverence. Now, we revere such a variety, such a number, of things and yet in the end they disappoint us. That Which *could* not disappoint us, That we *also* call G-d and *That* has to be prior; and insofar G-d has to be…

No more and no less power of proof than "Cogito ergo sum" ["I think, therefore I am"] does another proposition have: "*I love* (G-d), *therefore* (G-d) *is*". For just like the proposition that the act of thought implies the "I" as subject, so does the act of boundless love imply G-d, as the (infinite) Object.[8]

---

[8] It is true that instead of the *reflexive* self-reference of the act upon the subject, we have the *intentional* reference of the (intentional) act upon the transcendent *Object*, or better put, upon the *Transcendent* as object. Thereby, simultaneously the subjectivist or even solipsist limits on the world, indeed on the world-foundation or alternatively that which is beyond the world, are broken through. Thus, we see the following. When it is claimed that *anxiety* (not fear) opens existence ontologically (not ontically) to nothingness, then one is equally justified in claiming: *love* opens the human to the cosmos and its total unity. We could, however, go a step further and from "Cogito ergo sum" via the *"Amo ergo est"* [I love, therefore He is] reach an *"Amo ergo sum"* [I love, therefore I am]. For that we would need to continue with the following experience: everything becomes meaningful and the most extreme requirements become possible for a person, so long as he or she acts, tolerates or suffers *for the love of someone*. Thus, the person achieves the realization of his or her ultimate possibilities only in the *greatest* possible – in an unlimited – love. Unlimited love, however, can only be the love for a being worthy of infinite love. Such a being is called G-d. The more I love, the more I "am" (only in unlimited love do I reach the limits of my possibilities). However, all that I *can* be, I am, only when I love That which is worthy of the *greatest* love.

It is self-understood that any effort at a phenomenological proof will not be easy, for one who until now has had no experiential preparation, one who has closed himself – for the *person who "suppresses" his metaphysical need*. To be religiously persuaded, one would have to take in trust what can so be formulated: *could* there be a true *belief*, which *everybody* does not already *have*? Now this is not an absurd claim. For who, for example, does *not* believe in the You – the You of the next person. And isn't this You, as the spiritual bearer of the entire psychophysical organism, in fact *invisible*? Isn't the person of the other, as that core, which hides behind its psychophysical forms of manifestation and expression – that spiritual [identity], which the other person does not (as physical or mental) have, but rather precisely "is" – really totally imperceptible and only somehow graspable "behind" that which is outwardly perceived?

Now G-d – the *personal G-d* intended by the religious person – is ultimately nothing other, so to speak, than the primary You. Indeed, He is it, so much so, so essentially, that we cannot speak *of* Him in the third person, but rather only *to* Him, in the second person. I do not know, for example, whether it is possible for a person, who, let us say, was in a concentration camp and stood in the grave, to stand on a rostrum, in a lecture theatre, and speak *of* G-d, *as the same*, to Whom he spoke in the grave…

The character of religious experience

Now when existential analysis turns towards the religious modality of experience – to which it must address itself as one possibility, as one reality amongst the forms of human existence – and understands G-d as the primary You, then this has to do with a kind of primary image, or primary phenomenon and yet this phenomenon is not phenomenally given to perception! How is it possible? This too does not have to astound us, when we simply consider the forms of a daily experience, which provides a complete analogy: visual perspective. The perspective in a picture – the course of the so-called vanishing lines, which uniformly converge in a certain point – is thoroughly dominated by this point, known as the vanishing point. The point is virtual; it "is" not at all in the picture – in the very picture, which it in fact dominates. It is not actually represented in the picture. It does not itself appear in the picture, it is not at all "given" to perception and yet it is constitutive for the picture.

It is no different with that which we term values: they seem also to converge to a uniform point. And when we sufficiently consistently pursue these value-lines within existence, then in fact that point – transcendent and yet constitutive – in which these values lines converge, has to become manifest. It would be this point, this One, which unites all values. And perhaps the principal Jewish prayer – which consists of six Hebrew words [*Sh'ma Yisrael* (Hear, Israel) …] and states that the one G-d, is only one – in its deepest and ultimate meaning can be interpreted in this sense. At all events, it is *possible* to present all that is of value, as converging in a highest value, in a personification of value; so that perhaps every truth, ultimately conceived, means G-d; and every instance of beauty, ultimately loved, reveals G-d; and every greeting, rightly understood, greets G-d.

That the highest value, the highest personification of value, is accordingly not given to perception and yet somehow indeed given, is in itself no novelty. We know a very appropriate analogy for this from sensory physiology. It has been experimentally established that in the scaling of various intensities of a colour, let us say, red, the basis and departure point for comparison of various intensities of the colour is not the zero-point of the intensity scale, but much rather the one-hundred per cent saturated colour red, so to speak, the ultimate red. Never, however, does this make a phenomenal appearance. It never enters perception. Still it is asserted and is the presupposition of all comparisons of colour-intensities. We consequently hardly need to wonder, that in the area of values, we find something similar. As we know since Scheler, evaluation proceeds through preference or ranking of value-qualities, that is to say, in a manner of comparison. However, this comparison follows ostensibly from an, at all events, not given, but "asserted" supreme good (more actually, a personification of the highest good). In this sense – in this supposition – G-d would be the solution which preceded the riddle: He, Who set the riddle, instructed that the solution be found and let it be found.

The Absolute remains in transcendence. It is, and remains, there unreachable for all positivist apparent arguments, which might be raised against it. The religiously persuaded person, precisely because of his conviction, renounces outright the reasoning which moves both from one innerworldly being to another innerworldly being, as well as from the immanent world to the transcendent Absolute. This religiously persuaded person wonders little when he or she finds no proofs in innerworldly reasoning, no proofs, but rather at best encounters individual indications, which offer precious little to his reasoning, but all the more to his heart and his metaphysical heart's need. So it is also with "his" proofs in relation to a meaning for his existence and also in relation to those proofs, which bring him to *belief* in the meaning of his existence.

His question about the meaning of existence is thus quite differently meant than any answer which he could expect within or from the immanent world. He is not a psychic [who consults with spirits], since only psychics believe in spirits which answer them in words, or intervene into daily activity through "miracles" – vases hurled across the room and other such nonsense. These are spirits. But "Spirit" – or indeed *the* Spirit – does not answer. *For here all depends on asking.*

The religiously persuaded person will also really not be able to understand at all the metaphysician who, precisely in the old sense of ontic proofs and reasoning seeks to come to Being "in terms of its foundation". That *this* metaphysical departure, with such *ontic* means is doomed to failure from the outset, is evident from the following analogy –

When one wants to determine the depth of the ocean bed at any point the customary procedure is to undertake a sonic depth finding. It is no more than a prototype of the radar principle. Sound waves are sent down to the ocean floor and the time taken for the return of the echo is measured. Now, as stated, the metaphysician wants, as stated, to get to the basis of existence. *But existence has no floor.* And all our questions, precisely with regard to the ultimate basis of existence, find no echo in the unlimited ocean of being. But it is important to interpret this fact correctly and to ask, what kind of an Absolute would it be that without any more ado, stood available to speak and answer? And what kind of a strange infinity would it be if the voice – with which our ultimate questions are sent out into the infinite space of being – could be intercepted at its finite foundation walls. We know that no answer will come our way from the infinitely far and the infinitely deep foundation of being, *if we have correctly addressed our questions.* For we remain then without an answer precisely because our questions *have reached the infinite.*

The Absolute remains, as such, in transcendence. It is not "given" – at least not as something found. But it is given, as something sought. Nevertheless. Accordingly, it is never given its what-ness [i.e. what it is], but it is given in its that-ness [i.e. that it is]. It will accordingly not be a matter of finding the Absolute, along logical lines, as an ontic reality. But might it not have to do with the finding of a reality? Is there not, nevertheless, some such thing as the truthfulness of seeking? In this sense it could almost be asserted: there is only one truth, the great truth of belief, the truth of believing – the truthfulness in which belief is accomplished, in which it is lived as life.

The universality in religious experience

Until now, we have investigated, via an existential analysis, the religious modality of experience. Now, the question arises, whether beyond religious experience itself, something can be said from the standpoint of existential analysis, about what, in contradistinction, is called a creed [*Konfession* – a formal-traditional religious affiliation]? For one often hears people say, "I am religious; certainly, I believe in a G-d, but I do not feel myself *denominationally* bound".

Now it would certainly be going too far, a case of throwing out the baby with the bathwater, if – on account of symptoms of decadence and signs of decline – one wanted to designate the traditional religious affiliations together, with their institutions, as a kind of transcendental opportunism. For certainly, the *merely* traditionally-religiously affiliated person – who is really not religious – wants often, so to speak, only to insure himself for the eventuality that there *is* a G-d and a Beyond. However, one who thinks, that with this viewpoint they have located the truly religious person and authentic religiosity, is in error. For the truly religious person *is* not calculating or "weighing accounts". Precisely in opposition to the security-preoccupied bourgeois, he or she is much rather constantly preoccupied with being *accountable*.

In general, it seems to be most accurate to grasp the relationship of the individual positive traditional religious affiliations to pure religiosity entirely analogously to the relationship of the various national languages to "pure truth". A person comes to the truth only through thought, and in thought only via his or her particular language. "His" language, however, is a particular mother tongue – the language into the world of which he was born and in the particular traditional resources of which he grew up. Even if, without any doubt, one language is richer in nuance than another, nevertheless, he will *better and more closely* approach the intended *identical reality*, which hovers before all those differently speaking, through his own mother language.

One who, therefore, thinks that he must be without any particular traditional religious affiliation precisely for the sake of his religiosity is in error – just like one who thereby believes that this absence of traditional religious affiliation approaches a form of non-partisanship or impartiality. In terms of our analogy such a person, without traditional religious affiliation, would be none other than one who has no language. For *religious language* in general and for the average person is *only that of tradition-bound religious affiliation or it is nothing*.

Another point, however, arises from our analogy with language. Just as one cannot seriously entertain the thought that the natural languages could be simply supplanted by an artificial language, a "world language", even so nonsensical would be the concept of a general religion of humanity. For that would also necessarily be an "artificial religion", an artificial religiosity and hence none at all.

We have taken the following lesson from the analogy of language: the traditional religious affiliations intend somehow an identical primary reality. Nevertheless, their variety is a necessity for humanity. (Certainly, there are masters of translation from one language to another but they are surely the exception. There can be authentic and religiously fruitful conversions; but to promote them, from the standpoint of one particular traditional religion, from another or from all the other traditional religions, is not only unjust and unreasonable, but would also miss the point.)

It is albeit quite different when we ask, how the individual traditional religions – namely the monotheistic ones – in their individual beliefs can exist side by side, that is, be able to tolerate one another without "surrendering something". In this regard, it is clearly thinkable that the traditional religions join with one another in reciprocal understanding and tolerance through consciousness of the ultimate commonality of the common Ultimate insofar as they become aware of their commonality – that is the "monism of the monotheisms". But then the principal Jewish prayer, "Hear Israel, our (particular, personal) G-d is One", would have to open up to a "Hear, all nations (hear, all monotheistic religious traditions), the G-d (of our particular traditional faiths) is one, and one and the same!

The therapeutic rationale of drawing upon religion

Existential analysis was created with the intent of overcoming psychoanalysis, just as logotherapy was created to overcome psychologism within psychotherapy. It was contemplated first and foremost as a psychotherapeutic method of treatment. One will now ask, on what grounds should existential analysis therefore come to be at all concerned with the modality of religious experience, with the *Homo religiosus*? To this, a twofold answer is to be given.

First of all, existential analysis, as an interpretation of the human being – that is, as the anthropology, which it is – did not set out to exclude biologism and psychologism and sociologism from its doctrine of the essence of the human being, in order ultimately itself to fall into an anthopologism. It would have fallen into anthropologism, however, in the moment that it would make the human absolute, having previously relativized, making dependent, all ostensibly fated determinants of his biological, psychological and sociological "nature".

To make the human absolute, would be to conceive him or her as "just like G-d". One could, accordingly, if an anthropologically concerned existential analysis or alternatively an anthropologically oriented existential analysis would do this, *accuse such an anthropology of Theomorphism*, now that *theology* has enough been accused of *anthropomorphism*.

Now, we understand also, why ultimately existential analysis drew the "Absolute" into the debate. Within existential analysis, the Absolute is there only in order that the relative remain relativized –

We have learnt that the human givens (the being-so *[Sosein]* of the human) must be understood as being at the disposal of human freedom. But we have further learnt that this human freedom has a double aspect – one from below and one from above, one merely negative and one positive. For we have learnt to grasp freedom, not only as "freedom from", but also as "freedom to". As the "to what" of freedom, we have, however, imputed the assumption of responsibility. *Plainly, contemporary existentialism mostly sees only the "from what" of freedom*. It sees the human as an existence and this existence *as a possible being-free from specific, determinate being (Sosein)*, that is, freedom as possible confrontation of fate. But it has overlooked the fact, that *existence, most profoundly and ultimately, is being-responsible*! With the responsibility, however, which he or she undertakes, the person submits him- or herself – freely – to a law. Responsibility is thus even more so a binding-back together of freedom, a recoupling with a (higher) order in the sense of law. Binding-back together, in this sense, is – no less and no more – the literal translation [of the word] *re-ligio*.

When, therefore, for example, as Jean-Paul Sartre explains that the human has to discover the human, the first question is, whether and how this discovery of one's self can be carried out into nothingness, into the void – or whether, something must always be "presumed" by him – and, if so, what? Accordingly, if one does not hold simply to the phrase of Pascal, that the human can only be understood from the vantage point of G-d or the G-dly individual, one will still have to ask: How in Sartre's sense, could the person discover himself, if he had not already long discovered G-d, and perhaps only forgotten again?

We have given, as the first reason for drawing in the modality of religious experience into existential analysis, the relativization of the relative. Now, the second reason is a therapeutic or prophylactic one. For when we go even a little into the religious experience, we at once notice that this has to do plainly with the experience of one's own fragmentariness and one's own relativity in relation to an absolute background. In the religious self-conception, the person experiences his or her own relationship to the Absolute – that is, as to something which bears no relation! This paradox need not frighten us. For what else then is this-being-related-to something, which bears no relation than being hidden away – being hidden away in the Hidden, in the transcendent. Thus if we cannot solve this paradox, we can give it a positive application. In this positivity there is at once, from the psychotherapeutic or mental-health standpoint, an unheard-of value. For it is already evident that that the experience of life simply as a mission – one could say a personal mission – can raise the consciousness of responsibility to a degree which is eminently significant, psychotherapeutically. It becomes manifest pre-eminently how the religious experience, the experience of the Hidden comes to possess therapeutic relevance. At least in decisive moments of personal existence, it is repeatedly evident how hardly any other attitude in relation to fated border situations has the same power as the religious attitude, to allow a person to master these situations. Indeed, one is often tempted to say: We understand the suicide; we understand also the people, who do not believe in any higher meaning of their existence. What we do not really understand is why all those who do not believe in this higher meaning, do not commit suicide.

The neutrality of the therapist and the irreligious patient

To all appearances, it would seem at this point that all psychotherapy should merge into spiritual counselling. That is not the case[9]. For the doctor as such (mark my words: as such – that is to say, *not the particular doctor*, who as fellow believer, stands in a form of personal union with a patient from the same faith) is neither equipped as such, nor called upon to give a religious answer to the patient's question about the meaning of existence. He is not equipped because he is not there to assume the office of priest; and he is not called upon for this, since *neither* the religious *nor* the non-religious patient came to receive a religious answer *from him*. For the doctor, the religious patient has to be seen as placed equally with the non-religious patient. This has fundamental reasons and not simply historical ones, such as that associated with the phenomenon designated as the migration of humanity from the religious counsellor to the psychiatrist. As an historical fact, there is here nothing to discuss. From a medical standpoint, we have neither the right to investigate the causes of this fact, nor the right to ignore its consequences. We have much rather the obligation to

---

[9] It is a long time since one has an expectation of pure philosophy that it – of itself – consider itself the maidservant of theology. How unjust it would be to demand this specifically of medical psychology.

ask ourselves, what should or may happen with these "non-believing" people, who as a matter of fact come to us during consulting hours.

Already, it follows unambiguously, as mentioned at the beginning of our considerations in regard to the danger of a medical crossing-over of medical and competence boundaries, when it comes to the *Oktroi* of personal world-views, for the doctor only *[a] strict neutrality* is thinkable. *Existential analysis states only that the human being is on a search.* But it cannot by itself resolve *whether the search is for a G-d, whom the person invents, or on the search for the G-d, whom he or she does not find, or for the G-d, which he or she finds,* or *on the search for him- or herself.* This question is never answered simply from existential analysis, since G-d "is" not in a dimension to which existential analysis has access. Perhaps He is in no dimension, but rather is Himself the coordinate system.

Existential analysis has the task, at one and the same time to arrange the room of immanence without blocking the door to transcendence. The door remains open – that door, through which the spirit of religiosity can be brought in, or through which the religious person can go out, with all the spontaneity which belongs to all genuine religiosity.

Existential analysis thus by no means presents the end of the line for a person's ultimate discovery of meaning. For it *gives* no final answers, at least no *final* answers in the religious dimension. Yet, from that station, to which existential analysis can bring a person – regardless of whether he or she is religious or not – the person can without further ado also find a direct connection to *his final* destination. This happy circumstance will not surprise us: that the endpoint of the path of existential analysis follows the "route" to the religious. How true this is, can be seen in the manifold instances, in which existential analysis and a religious approach coincide. – Not long ago, it happened that a young female student, who had received a strict Catholic upbringing and was also personally committed to it, was directed by the Headmistress of her school to undergo outpatient psychotherapy. It was a case of severe psychological shock following rape. The despair of the patient had already led to suicidal thoughts. It was particularly tragic that this, virginal, young woman had already lost her fiancée in war. What was said to her in the framework of existential-analytic psychology, and with full psychotherapeutic efficacy, was shortly later found out to be almost literally identical with that which Augustine had expressed to some young Roman women in a similar situation.

However, a boundary crossing by psychotherapy – especially an existential-analytic logotherapy, that is "psychological pastoral counselling" – is not only illegitimate as therapeutically unnecessary, but from the point of religion *itself*, fully unnecessary. For it is ever evident, that the effect of an ultimate, that is, religious answer to the ultimate questions of the patient about the meaning of existence, is generally incomparably deeper when this answer – which can only come from a religious source – is *not* given, quasi lectured, by the doctor; but when the patient *alone* can say it to him- or herself. Again, we see how a strength emerges from the ostensible weakness of existential analysis: its limits grant it its prowess…

[A] strict *neutrality* is required of existential analysis; on the other hand, the factual experience is that of the so frequent *coincidence* between medical existential analysis and religious, pastoral procedures. Finally, there is the experience of the *spontaneous* breaking through of religiosity precisely on the part of patients, who have not been influenced in this regard in the course of medical treatment. From all of these facts, a single consequence can emerge for existential analysis as well as for psychotherapy vis-à-vis religious ministry: cooperation! And this becomes more effective, the more purely and cleanly the competencies are demarcated, instead of trying to encroach on one another's ground. The genuine possibility of such cooperation seems to us to be founded in that, following our conviction, at least in practice, that between the fundamental views of the religious and the non-religious there is no truly oppositional relationship. The relationship is not one of opposition, but addition. This can be seen most clearly, where the experience of life simply reveals itself as a mission, as the analogy of the religious person brought out – as no more and no less than *a step out*, simply beyond that sense of life as a task, which existential analysis posits as a psychotherapeutic goal. "A step out", however, is always only an *additional* step.

A human being, who in terms of his own person, has completed this step must never exhibit arrogance resulting from a sense of superiority over another, who has not fully pursued this way to its conclusion. For just as between the doctor and the clergyman there is only one requisite consequence – cooperation – so also between the religious and non-religious and especially between the religious of different traditional affiliations, there is a single consequence: tolerance!

Properly understood, tolerance has the least to do with liberalism and absolutely so with relativism. To interchange it with liberalism would make the true democratic spirit equal to liberalism. Democracy, however, has nothing to do with liberalism. Nevertheless, it extends validity to liberalism and must cooperate with it within a democratic system. For democracy validates itself precisely when it cooperates with something, with which it has nothing to do.

And when we now finally ask, how can I – insofar as I am one hundred per cent convinced of my belief – extend validity to another belief, to the conviction of another? Am I, by that very fact, untrue to my belief? We can only answer this question – which must be in the negative – when we consider the following. In the sense of authentic tolerance, I am tolerant of a different conviction and the belief of another, not because I in the slightest share something with him, but much rather because I respect him. And I respect him, because the belief of the other is after all the belief, the conviction of another, and because this other is precisely a human being and his conviction a human conviction and his belief, the belief of a person. As such, I must respect him. For I respect the belief of another not because I can share it, but rather because I must love the other person him- or herself.

TEN THESES CONCERNING THE 'PERSON'

Introductory paper for a discussion with
Professor Dr P. Ildefons Betschart OSB (Salzburg),
Dr Alois Dempf (Munich) and Dr Leo Gabriel (Vienna)
on the occasion of the Salzburg *Hochshulwochen* 1950.

Translated by Shimon Cowen

Whenever one speaks of a "person", one involuntarily associates with it another concept which intersects with it: the individual. Indeed, this is already the first thesis propounded here:

1. *The person is an individual [individuum]* in the sense of something indivisible: it cannot be subdivided or split, because it is a *unity*. Even in so-called schizophrenia – the "split-madness" – there is no real splitting of the person. So too in relation to other pathological conditions, there is no talk in clinical psychiatry of splitting of the personality, or nowadays of "double consciousness" but rather only of alternating consciousness. Even when Bleuler coined the concept of schizophrenia, he did not have in mind a true splitting of the person, so much as the splitting off of certain association complexes - a possibility which people then fascinated by the contemporary association psychology movement believed in at the time.

2. The person is not only an "in-dividual" [in the sense of indivisibility] but also not an undifferentiated aggregate *["in-summabile"]*. That is to say, a person is not only indivisible, but can also not be "melted down" [into a simple unity]. The reason for this is that [the person] is not just a unit but rather a [complex] whole. As such it is impossible for it to be assimilated to some higher order, such as "the mass", "class" or "race". All these unities or totalities, which subsume the person are not personal entities, but pseudo-personal in the highest degree. The person, who believes that he ascends [into his higher identity] in these in fact only founders and sinks. In becoming absorbed into the greater

group or category, he in fact surrenders himself as a person.

In contrast to the person, the organic realm is perfectly divisible and assimilable [capable of being "melted down"]. At least the well-known experiments of Driesch, carried out with sea-urchin eggs, have taught and demonstrated this. Moreover, divisibility and perfect assimilabilty are indeed the condition and presupposition of [organic] reproduction. From this in no way follows that the person as such is reproducible. It is only an organism, which can at a given time be reproduced, be created from older organisms. The person, the personal spirit – the spiritual existence – cannot be reproduced by man.

3. Every individual *person* is *absolutely unique [Novum]*. Thus, a father is in no way the creator nor, in the actual sense of the word, the engenderer of his child. He is much rather simply the instrument of a miracle, which constantly occurs with the entry into existence of a new human, a new person. This new person is created by G-d, and this not in the moment of "procreation", but rather as an act, accomplished by the Absolute, carried out beyond space and time – in a *nunc stans* [a "now" envisaged from eternity].

4. *The person is spiritual.* Thus, the spiritual person stands in heuristic and facultative opposition to the psychophysical organism. The organism is an ensemble of organs, that is, of instrumentalities. The function of the organism – the task, which it has to achieve for the person whom it bears (and by whom it is borne) – is in the first place an instrumental one. Beyond this, it is also an expressive one: the person needs its organism to be able to act and express itself. As a tool, which in this sense it is, the organism is a means to an end, and as such has a utility *[Nutzwert]*. The counter-concept of utility is that of dignity. Dignity, however, pertains alone to a person and does so essentially independently of all operative and social utility.

Only one who overlooks and forgets this, can justify euthanasia. One, however, who knows about the dignity – the unconditional dignity – of every single person, has unconditional respect for the human person, including the sick person – also for the incurably sick and the incurably mentally ill. In truth, there are really no *Geisteskranken* [literally, "sick of spirit", the term normally designating "mentally ill"]. For the spirit, the spiritual aspect of the person itself, cannot as a rule become sick. Even behind psychosis it is there, also when it is barely visible in the sight of the psychiatrist. I once designated this as the psychiatric credo: [namely,] the belief in the persistence of the spiritual person even behind the foreground symptoms of psychotic illness. For, as I said, were that not so, then there would be no point, as a doctor, to put the psychophysical organism in order, to "repair" it. For one who only sees the organism and not the underlying person, must be ready to perform euthanasia on an organism which has become irreparable, unless they see some other economic value in that life, as they would know nothing of the dignity of the person independently from that. This representation of what it means to be a doctor is that of the *médicin technicien* [doctor technician]. This kind of doctor, however, *médicin technicien*, with such thinking, betrays that for him, the sick person is an *homme machine* [a human machine].

Not only does sickness relate solely to the psychophysical organism and not to the spiritual person, but so also to the treatment. This applies to the question of lobotomy: not even the scalpel of the neurosurgeon – or, as it is nowadays called, the "psychosurgeon" – can touch the spiritual person. All that lobotomy can affect is to influence the psychophysical conditions, under which the spiritual person stands. And whenever the operation in question is indicated, these conditions will, in the long run, be improved. Accordingly, the indication of this intervention comes to a weighing of lesser and greater evils at the time. One has to weigh up whether the handicap, which could be established through the operation is less than that constituted by the illness. Then and only then is the intervention justified. In the end all medical action is connected with the inescapable necessity of sacrifice: that is, to pay with a lesser evil and to acquire the possibility of conditions, under which the person, no longer constrained and limited by the psychosis, can fulfil and realize himself.

Not only does physiology fail to address the person, but also psychology does not succeed in this – at least, when it submits to psychologism. To catch sight of the person or at least to do justice to the category [of a person] much rather requires a noology [a science of the spirit].

As known, there was [the mechanistic] "psychology without mind *[Seele]*", which has long been overcome. Contemporary psychology cannot, however, be spared the criticism of often being a psychology without spirit *[Geist]*. This spiritless psychology is, as such, not only blind to the dignity of the person, as well as to the person itself, but it is also value-blind. It is blind to those values, which on the world-scale correlate to those of individual personal existence. [It is blind to] the world of meaning and values, the ranking of values, and to values as an ordered world, a cosmos .[In short, it is blind] to the Logos.

Psychologism projects values out of the spiritual realm [where they have their own integrity] onto the mental plane, where they become ambiguous. On this plane, be it psychological or pathological, there can no longer be distinguished the visions of a Bernadette from the hallucinations of an hysterical woman. I normally give over this notion to my students in lecture courses by pointing to the fact that from the similar two-dimensional circular base outline of a three-dimensional ball, cone and cylinder, one can no longer see what one is dealing with. In psychological projection, conscience becomes superego or alternatively, the "introjection" of the "father image", and G-d becomes the "projection" of this image. The fact is, however, that this psychoanalytic interpretation itself represents a projection - a psychologistic [projection].

5. *The person is existential.* This means that [the person] is not a [datum, a] fact, which exists within the realm of facts, facticity. The human, as person, rather than being a datum is a being possessed of facultative capacities. It exists at any time in terms of its own possibility, for or against which it can decide. The being of a human, as Jaspers characterized it, is "deciding" being. One decides at any time, what will be in the next moment. As deciding being, it diametrically opposes the representation [of the human] in psychoanalysis as instinct-driven being.

As I have always characterized it, to be human is to be profoundly and ultimately responsible. With this is clearly implied that [existential] means more than simply being free. In responsibility, the goal of human freedom is also given: to what a human is free, for what or against what one decides. These are specifically the world of meaning and values, the scale of values and the pivot or summit of every value hierarchy: G-d.

In the perspective of an existential analysis, as I have attempted to formulate it, the person, contrary to psychoanalysis, is not instinct-driven, but rather meaning-oriented; contrary to the psychoanalytic perspective not oriented towards desire, but towards values. In the psychoanalytic conception of sexual drive (libido) and the notion of social connectedness (the sense of community) found in individual psychology, all we see is the deficient, if not decadent, modality of a more primary phenomenon: love. Love is forever the relationship between an "I" and a "you". In psychoanalytic perspective all that remains of this is the *Id* – sexuality – and in that of individual psychology, a ubiquitous sociality: the "they" *[das "Man"]*.

Whilst psychoanalysis sees human existence as ruled by a will to pleasure and individual psychology by a will to power, existential analysis views it as dominated by a will to meaning. It knows not only a struggle for existence and, beyond this at most, mutual help (Peter Kropotkin), but also a struggle for the meaning of existence – with mutual support in this struggle. Essentially that support is what we call psychotherapy. It is essentially *médicin de la personne* [treatment of the *person*] (Paul Tournier). From this it is clear that the concern of psychotherapy is ultimately not the redirection of emotional dynamics or instinctual energies, but rather an existential reorientation.

6. *The person is essentially an "I"* rather than "it": not subject to the dictate of the Id [bodily being], a dictatorship, which Freud may have had in mind, when he asserted that the "I" is not master in its own house. The person, the "I", is not led by the Id, by instinctual drives, whether dynamically or genetically. The notion of the *driven* I, as a contradiction in terms, is wholly to be rejected.

Indeed, the person also has an unconscious dimension, but that is precisely where the spiritual has its root. Precisely in its primary source, [the spiritual] is not only in terms of its facultative capacity, but also *necessarily*, unconscious. In its source and foundation, the spirit is unreflected and so unconscious pure agency. Accordingly, we must distinguish very carefully between that instinctual unconscious, with which alone psychoanalysis is concerned, and the spiritual unconscious. To unconscious spirituality belongs also unconscious belief, unconscious religiosity: an unconscious and not uncommonly repressed innate relationship of the human being to transcendence. It was the merit of C.G. Jung to have illumined that. His error, however, was to localise this unconscious religiosity where unconscious sexuality is to be localised, in the instinctual unconscious of the Id. To belief in G-d and to G-d Himself I am alone not driven. Rather I have to decide for or against Him. Religiosity is the province of the "I" or nothing.

7. The person is not simply unity and totality (see 1 and 2, [above]) but *establishes* unity and totality. It establishes the body-mind-soul unity and totality, which represents the "human". Only the person establishes, founds and assures this unity and totality; only the person constitutes, establishes and guarantees it. Generally, we humans recognize the spiritual person only as coexistent with its psychophysical organism. At least this applies to the person, while he or she lives, *intravital*, not *postmortal*. One, for whom the person is wholly identified with the body-mind-soul unity and totality, submits the spiritual to human mortality. Only when the person is grasped as [intrinsically] spiritual, is it lifted out of the mortality of the psychophysical[1].

---

[1] The objection [to this] that *post mortem* the (resurrected) person receives a different (transfigured) body can easily be answered. This body is certainly not identical with the original one. Much rather this new body is pure, unsullied expression of the person. The "beautiful soul" receives an equally beautiful body. The new body is purely expressive

Whilst [a person] lives, the psychophysical cannot be detached from the spiritual; both are inseparably bound up with one another. The human represents a point of intersection, a junction of the three planes of existence: body, mind and soul[2]. These planes of being cannot be clearly distinguished from one another (Cf Jaspers, N. Hartmann). Nevertheless, it would be false to say that the human is "constructed" from body, mind and soul. It is unity and totality, but within this unity and totality, the spiritual in the human confronts its bodily and mental aspects. It is this which constitutes what I once called the noo-psychic antagonism. Whilst the parallel psychophysical side is a binding one, the noo-psychic one is facultative. It is only ever possibility; simply, a power *(Mächtigkeit)* – albeit a power to which appeal can constantly be made, and to which therapy must appeal. Forever the task remains to summon the defiant power *(Trotzmacht)* of the spirit, as I have called it, against the psychophysical, which seems so powerful. Psychotherapy in particular cannot dispense with this summons. This I have characterised as the second – the psychotherapeutic – credo: namely, the belief in this ability of the soul within the human, somehow, under all conditions and circumstances to pull back from its psychophysical dimensions and to assume a productive distance from it. [Imagine], contrary to the first *psychiatric* credo, that it were not the task to repair the psychophysical organism because [it were thought that] the spiritual person, whole despite all sickness, did not yearn for it. Then we would not be in a position, as the second credo requires, to summon the spiritual in the human as a power of resistance against the bodily-mental dimension within it, inasmuch as this noo-psychic antagonism would not exist.

8. *The person is dynamic.* Inasmuch as the person can distance and elevate itself from the psychophysical, does the spiritual emerge into manifestation. We cannot [therefore] hypostasize [- delimit -] the spiritual person because it is dynamic. For that reason [too], we cannot qualify it as a "substance", certainly not as substance in any *received* sense of the word.

---

of that which [the soul] is, so that that would be "written on the body".

[2] One could naturally equally speak of "dimensions" as well as planes (*Ärtzliche Seelsorge*, p. 140). To the extent that the spiritual dimension primarily and only belongs in the human, is it the distinctive dimension of human existence. If the human is projected out of the space of the spiritual, in which he essentially exists, into the planes of the merely mental or even physical, so has one sacrificed not only one, but *the* human dimension (*Die Leib-Seele-Geist-Problematik vegetativer und endokriner Funktionstoerungen*, 2. Lindauer Psychotherapiewoche [in print]). Compare Paracelsus: "Only in the heights of the human does the human exist".

9. *An animal is not a person*, because it cannot elevate itself above itself, or take up a position against itself. That is why the animal does not have the correlate of the person: it has no world, but only a [conditioning] environment. Extrapolating from the animal-human relation or environment-world, we arrive at the personal G-d and His "world"-correlate, the "super world". As the highest spiritual being facing the human being, G-d is no less than person - in reality, super-person. All statements about Him accordingly can be meaningful only be by way of analogy.

10. *The person is* to be understood finally as *the likeness of G-d*. The human can comprehend him- or herself only from the perspective of transcendence. The human *is* human only insofar as he grasps himself in relation to G-d. He *is* a person only in the measure that he personifies transcendence: tuned and resonant with the summons of transcendence. The summons of transcendence is heard in the conscience. The conscience is the registry of transcendence.

As little as a human being is what he or she is in the dimension of immanence [simply being in the world], so little does he [within that perspective] experience what he should be: he is thus unable to "project" *[entwerfen]* and "discover" himself, as an atheistic existentialism imagined he can. The true discovery of the human, the *inventio hominis*, occurs in the *imitatio Dei* [the imitation of G-d].

PSYCHOLOGICAL AND
PASTORAL COUNSELLING

Translated by Liesl Kosma

The German psychiatrist, Viktor E. von Gebsattel, once spoke of Western man's move away from the religious mentor to the psychiatrist. The fact can be regretted and an attempt made to counteract it: where, for example, one is a psychiatrist in a case where the patient is obviously more in need of spiritual guidance, that patient should also be referred on to a religious mentor. Experience in professional medical practice, however, has shown time and time again, as another German psychiatrist, Dr. Heyer, once said: those people who turn to us psychiatrists, not because of an illness in the literal sense, but because of a spiritual crisis, do not even want to be referred on to the theologian by the psychiatrist. Rather, they insist on being helped also in this spiritual crisis (which may not necessarily coincide with mental illness). What these people wish and yearn for – what they demand of the psychotherapist – is that he try to lift their spiritual crisis off its hinges. In these cases, such people are not served by the psychotherapist fobbing them off with bromides; or who pours on valerian drops to drown a person's intellectual struggle with the meaning of existence – with the concrete and personal meaning of his own life, that is, with the "metaphysical" need of man. It is, therefore, not really the case in this situation, that various philosophical problems have been carried over into psychotherapy; it is more that those patients are going to their therapist with questions about their own approach to life. If some individual therapist, through these questions, is perhaps driven into a corner, then the art of psychological healing itself, of psychotherapy, is similarly pushed into a new domain of problems.

This is no easy problem. The personal questions of an approach to life, which a person now imposes on the therapist do not in themselves present an illness so much as something essentially human. Indeed, this is the uniquely human condition (since an animal, for example could certainly never put to itself the question of the meaning of its existence). It all depends on the therapist's not misunderstanding this *essentially* human condition as only something all *too* human, as say a weakness or complex and the like. To the contrary, it is essentially the task of therapy, at least of modern psychotherapy, that the deep yearning of man for meaningful existence be taken as its starting and focal point in order to insert the therapeutic lever and precisely to appeal to that which I have called the "will to meaning". For what Nietzsche once said is true, and must be repeated time and again: "He who has a Why to live for can tolerate nearly every How". That is to say, he who knows the meaning of his existence is best able to overcome any difficulties.

It goes without saying that a purely psychoanalytic point of view would scarcely uncover such a concept as a will to meaning. There is no room for it in the psychoanalytic view of man. Psychoanalysis sees man more or less exclusively from the point of view, and in relation to, his drives; and that authority which comes forward against these drives and turns against them – be it to suppress, censure or to sublimate them – this authority too is itself derived from drives, and leads back to drives. In other words, that in man which does not consist of instinctual energies, at least derives from them. On the other hand, contrary to this view of man, the Swiss psychiatrist, Boss, for example, has correctly pointed out that such a deeply human delving personality of genius as that of Freud could not in the least be itself "explained" in terms of simple instinctual energies. But Freud himself would probably today be opposed to such one-sided and exclusive perspectives in the conception of the nature of man. Wasn't it Freud himself, who, already even in his lifetime said that man is mostly not only in reality more immoral than he thinks but also much more moral than he thinks. Well, I would like to allow myself to add the following: not uncommonly, man is also unconsciously much more religious in his Unconscious than he suspects. For not only are there unconscious, let us say suppressed, drives, but there are also unconscious spirituality, unconscious morality and unconscious faith. Of course, one should not make the same mistake as Jung fell into, by presenting such unconscious religiosity as inborn, as connected with the brain and so in turn merely instinctual. Rather, like all religiosity so also this unconscious faculty has somehow the quality of personal decision.

What the greatest psychotherapeutic classic – Freud – had to say on the topic of religiosity would probably scarcely satisfy the psychotherapist of today.

It is well known that Freud held religion to be an illusion, or, on another occasion, as a collective obsessional neurosis of humanity. It was his opinion that G-d was after all the figure of the father projected into superhuman dimensions, or, to stay with the jargon of psychoanalysis, a "father image". In the meantime, no less a figure than Karl Jaspers, one of the most significant philosophers of the present day, and originally a psychiatrist by profession, described psychoanalysis as a psychotherapeutic movement which had grown to become a confused world-view. It is known that this world-view has nowhere today penetrated more widely or deeply into mass consciousness than in the United States. Accordingly, Freyhan, an American psychiatrist, could write not so long ago in a Swiss professional journal, that psychoanalysis in the USA represented a mass movement which, with a kind of religious simplicity (that is, with a tendency to simplify), believed the source of all human actions and dealings to have been found in the all-powerful sphere of the unconscious. Indeed, in the basic tenets of psychoanalysis, at least in the old school, the so-called orthodox school, we can find much more that is reminiscent of unproven (because they are unprovable) articles of faith than scientific hard facts. It is widely true to say of this psychoanalysis, at least, that it is a belief which believes itself to be a science.

Who should therefore be surprised, when true belief, religion, the creed of one or another of its leading representatives, were occasionally to raise its voice in warning to point out how psychoanalysis without knowing – or even wanting – is the basis of a distorted view of man: mind you, a view of man which does not emerge from factual research but is already taken for granted in all psychological research. A few years ago, an American researcher, named Kristol, showed that is not possible to recognize results of psychoanalysis; and one can only deny its view of man, its depiction of man as not really a spiritual but rather an ultimately instinctual being. Kristol proved further that the two are closely linked, so that one can only either believe in a G-d or in the father image[1]. A warning was given repeatedly about the world-view implications – that is, of underestimating what in terms of a world-view is – involved in psychoanalysis, however unconscious it might itself be. One can appreciate this warning when we see how many psychoanalysts, themselves thoroughly believing individuals, try to criticize psychoanalysis. They do it with only half

---

[1] Compare W. Ginsburg and J.L. Herma: "Most analysts would question the results of their therapy in a patient who persisted in his religious practices at the end of an analysis" (*American Journal of Psychotherapy* 7, 546, 1953).

measures – I would say, they wash the fur of psychoanalysis, but don't get it wet, only sprinkling it with "holy water".

With all that, it should not be said that scientific research must wait until it is accredited by religion – judged and recognized. For we have been speaking of psychoanalysis in this very respect – we criticized it only to the extent – that it does not in fact represent pure research but rather believes itself to be science whilst, in reality, it is a kind of belief, more to the point, a superstition; more exactly: the superstitious belief in the instinctual in man as the origin and essence of everything human altogether. However, not only does scientific research have absolutely nothing at all to do with religion, this applies also and foremost to the therapist's practice. J.H. Schultz (of Berlin) recently could rightly dare to say in a German medical weekly publication: that as little as there can be a Christian or Buddhist obsessional neurosis, so little can there be a religiously determined scientific psychotherapy, mind you: *scientific* psychotherapy.

We want, however, to ask the further question: should the psychotherapist of today endeavour to attend to the spiritual need of his patient and the world-view issues which today's patient so often brings to him - so often specifically to him and no longer to the religious counsellor? Has this attempt at spiritual counselling to satisfy the role forced on him of "doctor of the soul" not brought a convergence of psychotherapy with religion, and the therapist with the religious mentor? Has this convergence not conjured up a blurring of the borders, confusion of tasks and misjudging of goals? In response we must confess that the danger of stepping over each other's lines is not inconsiderable. But for that very reason, to be able to respect each other's borders, it is imperative first to establish these limits. I must say that the drawing of boundaries between psychotherapeutic and spiritual care appears, at closer inspection, to be so clear and sharp that one can only be amazed at how often these boundaries are over-stepped.

What then is the task of psychotherapy, the healing of mental conditions, psychological counselling? Its goal is psychological healing, the restoration of psychological balance. What, on the other hand, is the aim of religion, of spiritual care, care of the soul in its literal sense? Something quite different: namely, not psychological healing or the maintenance of psychological equilibrium, but purely and solely spiritual help. Where religion, however, is concerned with this spiritual guidance, there is also the danger that the psychological equilibrium of the person can be shaken, that is, there is the danger that the person can experience psychological tension or be thrown into inner conflict.

So much for the differing tasks and goals of psychotherapy and religion. But note well: whilst religion is primarily and originally not concerned with the maintaining of psychological balance, it appears time and again how often religion – without even intending it – can in fact profoundly and incomparably contribute much to the maintenance of psychological equilibrium; so indeed, that it offers the person a psychological anchor and security, which he has simply been unable to find anywhere else. However, as mentioned, this occurs not by intention, but by the way.

And we see something analogous on the other side, that of psychotherapy. Again, without it having been intended, without psychotherapy having wanted or even having be allowed to want it, it happens again and again: *that in the course of psychotherapeutic treatment the mentally ill person harks back to the blocked-up spring of primary belief* – precisely to that unconscious religiosity which I spoke of earlier! But whenever such a thing should happen, it should not be the intention of psychotherapy - it must not be a goal, which hovers before the psychotherapist. It is not the task of his procedure, only an outcome.

If, in specific cases, it comes to this occurrence, we should not interpret it as success achieved by the doctor, but only as grace, which occurs to the patient.

THE SCIENCE OF THE SOUL

Selections from Viktor Frankl's Contributions to
a Dialogue with Pinchas Lapide[1]

Translated by Shimon Cowen[2]

The religious orientation of the human being[3]

I like to say that logotherapy is open – and indeed its hallmark is its openness
– to a dimension which other schools of psychotherapy are not. This is the
theological dimension, which encompasses the anthropological dimension and
therefore also psychotherapy [which is within the anthropological dimension].
In this sense, the hierarchical position of mental health is not only different
from that of spiritual health [afforded by theology]. The objectives of psychotherapy and religion are also found on different planes. In other words, the
plane to which the religious person advances is different from that on which
psychotherapy functions.

Why then do I use the word "dimension"? This word is meant to emphasize
not a formal ontological distinction between theology and psychotherapy, but
rather what I call a relationship of inclusion. In English, one says: "The higher
dimension is the more inclusive one". That is to say, between these individual
dimensions, there is not mutual exclusivity, but, to the contrary, a relationship of inclusion. Put differently, the truth of the one can never contradict the

---

[1] *G-ttsuche und Sinnfrage, op. cit.*

[2] The captions (including the title given to this translation) and the explanatory insertions
– which are all the bracketed additions within the translation – are those of the translator.
All footnotes are also those of the translator: both those giving the page numbers from
the German original for the selections and those providing further explanation.

[3] *G-ttsuche und Sinnfrage*, pp. 51-52.

truth of the other [or psychology is situated within the wider framework of theology]. Indeed, the fact is, that only within the higher dimension is the specific reality of the lower dimension illuminated.

To make this more concrete, let me give an example. Take a non-religious person, a non-believer, who simply follows his or her conscience. This person understands conscience as the final point of consultation. This is in contrast to the religious person, who sees behind conscience a higher authority, namely the Divine. Now this atheist, who follows his or her conscience will never come into conflict with the truth of the religious person. The reason for this is that the [transcendent] religious "world" – if I may put it this way – includes the innerworldly realm [of the spiritually unaware mundane] within itself. There can be no contradiction between them [where both are engaged in self-transcendence according to their stages]. Consequently, I speak of "dimensions", because this term emphasizes their essential difference as well as their coherence and inclusivity...

Indeed, we must pursue this recognition to the point that we take it as fact that the human being is a fundamentally religious being. Throughout history, the human being has remained a religious being and only in recent centuries has religion been watered down, though it has certainly not disappeared. The reason for its non-disappearance is that the human being is, as ever, unconsciously religious. There is an expression of Freud: "Not only is the human being in his unconscious not non-moral, but rather many times over more moral than he consciously imagines". We could vary, or extend, this statement to read: "In the unconscious, the human being is far more religious than he or she consciously imagines".

G-d or my innermost self?[4]

Religion has to do with G-d, and the religious person turns, when he or she speaks religiously, to G-d. Who [is this G-d], to Whom one turns? I have personally recently come to an operational definition of G-d. What does "defining operationally" mean? We come across an example of this in measuring intelligence quotients. Intelligence is that which is measured through *this* test. One cannot say what intelligence *is*. That is immensely difficult. Rather, we have to agree that what is now being measured ["intelligence"] is operationally defined by the "hands and feet" of this test. Now, in relation to G-d (– I was fifteen years old, when I

---

[4] *Ibid.*, p. 69.

sensed this definition –): "G-d" is the partner of the most intimate discussions which we hold with ourselves. Now, are these discussions with ourselves really discussions being held with *ourselves*, or in fact dialogues with *another* – with *the completely Other*[, G-d]? It does not matter if the question remains open.

Who[5] can say that he or she is a "believer"? I don't know if I can say that I am a believer. However, one can only gain an appreciation of the relative meaninglessness of a formulaic "statement" of belief in G-d, when one has once lived in one's fullest humanity. I know [in the concentration camp] where the SS-guard stood – in front of which barracks... [a]nd deep in my inner being, I was thinking – and I don't recall with which words – "Did *you* see? Look at that". That helpless upward gaze...

Was I then speaking to myself, or to G-d? No one overheard me. Something utterly honestly rebelled, resisted within me: "How could this be?" I despair. Inwardly I cry out – to whom do I cry out? To me – to Frankl – to myself, or to G-d? Maybe I did at that moment in the concentration camp say, "G-d, did You see that?" I don't remember. But whatever you call it – whether "G-d" or not – is a secondary question.

In recent years[6] I have again been coming around to something I once thought when I was fourteen, or at most fifteen, years old. I have in mind the definition of G-d which makes the Infinite finite, which reduces G-d down *(de-finitio)* to that which is the partner of my most intimate discussions with myself. When one – even an atheist – conducts the most intimate discussions with oneself, holds dialogue with oneself – and 'most intimate' means with absolute honesty and absolute openness, without concern for anything else, when we truly do not delude ourselves – one has the right to call this or that, to which one has turned, G-d. I am convinced that should G-d really exist, he won't mind if someone mistakenly exchanges Him for that person's true self and thus misnames Him.

The atheist will simply reply, "It's a joke [to call it G-d]. I'm only talking to myself". The Freudian psychoanalyst will say, "We're in dialogue with our Superego". Another will say, "We are speaking with our conscience". And the religious person will say simply, "I call that, G-d".

In other words, the irreligious person is one who accepts his or her conscience as a fact within psyche, coming to a virtual halt before this fact as

---

[5] This and the next paragraph are from *ibid.*, p. 94.

[6] The rest of this selection is from *ibid.*, p. 97.

something limited to the world. In truth, one can say that this halt is a premature one, because that person regards conscience as the end of the line, as the final authority to which one has to answer. The conscience is not really the ultimate authority before which I have to answer, but rather the penultimate one. The conscience is telling me *for what* I have to answer, but not *before Whom*.

And I believe that this – before Whom we stand – is not only a reality, but rather a supra-personal being, a Higher-than-Person, which at the very least must become internalized as [the individual's own] person [i.e. as conscience]. What is wrong with that?

The objectivity of ethics[7]

With regard to the question of relativism, I believe in an *objectivity* of truth, in an objective ethical imperative in each momentary concrete situation encountering us. At the same time, I believe also in "relativity", but in a sense different to that in which philosophers commonly speak of relativity. Indeed, I believe in objective truth and objective values; yet these are always relative, in the specific sense of being relative to the particular person and the particular situation.

Karl Jaspers expressed this very beautifully when he said that the more universally valid – that is, valid for a greater number of people – a value is, the more does its stringency and obligatoriness vary. In the Ten Commandments, for example, it is stated, You shall not steal[8], You shall not bear false witness, You shall not commit adultery nor covet your neighbour's wife. These are general values which were given to all humanity. According to Jaspers, we should now expect that they will sometimes lose their obligatoriness – because [and notwithstanding that] they are universal. It is because they are absolute and claim absolute validity, that one can overlook their relativity to concrete situations.

Let me give you an example. In the concentration camp, the meaningful thing to do in the concrete circumstances – what we used to call "organizing" – was to steal a piece of dough, a couple of potatoes. Anyone

---

[7] *Ibid.*, pp. 58-60

[8] The prohibition of theft is stated once in the Ten Commandments (Exodus 20:15) and again in Leviticus (19:11). The first refers to stealing – abducting – persons; the second to stealing property. Frankl here places them together, as indeed they are included together in universal Noahide law – the group of laws promulgated at Sinai for all humanity – under the common rubric of the prohibition of theft.

who pulled this off was proud and had absolutely no sense of having done something immoral. Thus, the application of this Commandment is relative: there are circumstances [such as the starvation we faced in the concentration camp] where the ethical requirement of the situation for me is that I steal.

Another example. You shall not bear false witness. Under Hitler, I succeeded in saving Jews from euthanasia. This was possible because I discovered that a Jewish old age home had vacant beds, of which the Gestapo happened not to know. The Director of the old age home provided assurances that no mentally ill persons would be accepted. However, we came to a tacit arrangement with my fatherly friend, Professor Otto Pötzl – who was then Head of the Vienna Psychiatric University Clinic – that every Jewish patient would be immediately transferred to the Jewish old age home. All we had to ask the home was, "We have a Jewish patient – will you take him?" and the answer was, "Yes". No one ever mentioned that he had a psychosis. As soon as he arrived there, I would receive a call. I had to get into a Taxi, travel there and write a false testimonial – that he had no psychosis. Out of schizophrenia I made a speech palsy resulting from concussion and out of depression I made a delirium induced through fever. I put my head in the noose, but I assumed that none of the supervisors would be clever enough to pick these up. I gave Cardiazol shock therapy to these psychotic patients who were brought to the Jewish old age home and a few weeks later they were discharged, free of all symptoms – and their lives were saved. I gave false testimony, but I would have been immoral (under the threat of their euthanasia) had I not done so. I had to take this responsibility upon myself.

And a third example from the Commandments: You shall not commit adultery. The last words that I said to my first wife, when we were forced to part at Auschwitz, were: "Stay alive at all costs. Do you understand me, at all costs?". With that, I absolved her in advance of any guilt in committing adultery in circumstances that should she have to prostitute herself to an SS-man (who would have killed her had she refused[9]). I did not want to have any guilt in her death by leaving her in uncertainty and doubts that "I cannot do this to Viktor", "What would Viktor think, if he knew?", "What would he say?" etc.

---

[9] It should be noted here that under universal, Noahide law one may commit adultery to save one's life. Under Jewish law, there is an ethical imperative to martyr oneself rather than commit adultery, but one who succumbs under this extreme duress – threat to life – and does commit adultery is not punished for doing so. Even in the case of extreme duress, there is a distinction between a male's conduct, which is an action, and a female's, which is wholly passive.

There I gave her an advance absolution, so as not to share guilt in her death. Three times a law of the Ten Commandments was contradicted [as indeed universal ethics from Sinai provides in such circumstances].

Notwithstanding this, these commandments are, were and remain general commandments applying across history and across societies. And yet for all that, in individual circumstances precisely they do not apply. That is to say, in general one should not steal, bear false witness or commit adultery. However, when it comes to "meaning" (that is, ethical purpose), as I understand it in the framework of logotherapy – as this confronts the concrete unique person and the concrete momentary situation – one must speak of *concrete* meaning. Values – and also commandments – are, in other words, general guidelines for conduct. Ethical purpose is something concrete, because each person is unique and each situation is unique and concrete [warranting on occasion special application of universal principles].

The basis of self-actualization[10]

Self-actualization is possible only to the extent that I lose myself, forget myself, overlook myself. For I need to have a reason, a foundation upon which I actualize myself. That foundation consists in devoting myself to an ideal or person... When I no longer keep that person or ideal in sight – which is what I am about, and instead the focus is on me, alone – in that moment I lose the basis upon which to actualize myself. The entire focus is then upon self-actualization *itself.* It is exactly the same thing with the striving for happiness or for the fulfilment of a desire. When I have no reason for happiness, I can't be happy. Accordingly, when I strive just to be happy, I lose sight of everything which could give me a reason to be happy. The more I pursue happiness, the more I chase it away. To understand that, one has to get beyond the common assumption that a person exists only in order to be happy. What a person really wants is a *reason* to be happy. Only once a person has a reason for it, does happiness enter – indeed follows automatically. To the same degree, however, that I focus on happiness, do I lose sight of the reason which I could have for happiness. Then happiness slumps and indeed cannot be roused. In other words, happiness must come as a consequence, not as a goal in itself.

The same applies to self-actualization. One, who makes "self-actualization"

---

[10] *Op. cit.*, 63-64.

his or her essential goal, overlooks the fact that one realizes one's ultimate purpose only to the extent that one – out there, in the world – accomplishes an ethical value. In other words, self-actualization ceases to preoccupy one, to the extent that – like happiness – it is grasped as the by-product of fulfilment of an ethical value.

So, it is not about "self-actualization" in, and for, itself, but rather about becoming oneself along one's path through the world, via those ideals and people in the world, whom I feel must matter to me.

The G-d beyond reason[11]

What is G-d? All our statements about G-d have to be understood as standing in quotation marks: "G-d is of a personal nature", "G-d is kind" and so forth. Anthropomorphisms are unavoidable. What matters is that we are aware that these *are* anthropomorphisms. That is the important thing. We cannot circumvent or avoid them. The attributes ascribed to G-d are and remain human attributes and often enough they are all-too-human attributes. G-d is not spared being symbolized in an anthropomorphic manner and form. But can we, on account of these all-too-human features, be justified in discarding everything religious? Is it not far more likely that what must anyway be an asymptotic approach to the secret and paradox of ultimate truth – G-d – will be more productive, when pursued in a symbolic rather than in an abstract way?

In this connection, Max Scheler states that none of the anthropopathic features – "G-d is angry", "G-d rages", "G-d has pity" – applied to G-d [Himself] are valid. Nevertheless, he says that with these we reach the G-d of prayer, as he calls it. We catch more of the truth – the theological truth – through the personified G-d of prayer, than through an abstractly and metaphysically grasped G-d as *ens realissimum* (a metaphysically conceived "most real being") and the like. This idea is also intimated in the saying of Pascal, "What interests me is the G-d of Abraham, Isaac and Jacob".

Perhaps I might most particularly shock you, were I to say to you, as Konrad Lorenz – I think in a television discussion with Franz Kreuzer – explicitly stated: "The peasant's wife, from some farm in the hills, who sees G-d as a man with a white beard, and various other primitive anthropomorphisms, is still much closer to the truth than any scientist". With that he is getting at exactly what we are saying.

For many, who regard themselves as atheists, this anthropomorphism is

---

[11] *Ibid.*, pp. 71-72.

foolish and irritating. One gets over this irritation, when one learns to acknowledge that one cannot actually escape anthropomorphism.

But I ask you[12], why can't G-d also allow Himself a "white beard", instead of being "clean shaven"? Why shouldn't G-d – as Konrad Lorenz wanted to say, or Max Scheler meant when he spoke of the "G-d of prayer", or in my sense of the justification of the wildest anthropomorphisms, if need be – also take on the form of a father, become the Papa, the grandfather, the "grandfather-image", as I once called it? Why shouldn't He be allowed to do that – in order to come down to the lowest level of intellectualization [which also, significantly and requisitely, is] the highest level of de-intellectualization [– freedom from the *constraints* of intellect]?

When[13] people object to religion that its concepts are all-too anthropomorphic, one can just as well counter that numerous concepts in physics – such as "force" and "matter" – are no less anthropomorphic. Notwithstanding this, these words stay in our vocabulary – indeed, our scientific vocabulary. Just like Scheler's statements about the G-d of prayer, they are figurative and allegorical and nonetheless they are somehow valid[14].

There are also those atheists, who became atheists "after Auschwitz", like Rubinstein and others. We hear it asserted that it is impossible to write poetry after Auschwitz; and that even less can one believe in G-d after Auschwitz.

One "option" is to give up one's belief in G-d from a vantage point, which we find so expressed in Dostoyevsky: "When G-d can allow that a single innocent child must suffer, let alone die, I cannot believe in Him". Alternatively, one preserves one's belief – so to speak, *despite* this. We say "Yes", despite it. And, indeed, this is for the simple reason that I utterly dispute that one can bargain and say: "Dear G-d, listen here. Up

---

[12] This paragraph is taken from *ibid.*, pp. 86-87.

[13] *Ibid.*, pp. 72-73.

[14] It should be noted that there are some attributes which we ascribe to G-d, such as those used in Scripture: "merciful", "kind", "judging" and so forth. These are the attributes, which indeed the soul also possesses, and through which it is possible to "imitate" G-d. That is to say, these attributes are not merely humanly ascribed, but have a theological validity. Even so, these attributes – which Scripture and tradition state – were themselves are created by G-d [rather than inhering in G-d Himself]. They form a spiritual template through which the soul of the human being (made in the image of the Creator) also possesses and via which the human can relate to, and "imitate", the Creator. When, however, we pray to G-d, we pray "to *Him* and not to His attributes", as tradition requires of us.

to 526,000 gassed Jews I will continue to believe in You – but not one more. Because You allowed five or six million to die, I withdraw my belief". One can't bargain. Take note: belief – real belief – goes beyond that. How many people do we hear saying, "Most people in Auschwitz must have lost their belief"? But it is not true. I have no statistics, but my own impression[15], my own feeling, is that in Auschwitz more people recovered their belief, and there were more in whom belief was strengthened, than lost their belief. We should therefore stop constantly working the formula of "after Auschwitz" in relation to the ability to believe. Rather, we should talk of belief *despite* Auschwitz.

This[16] is like what I experienced, shortly before the liberation from the concentration camp, with Gabriel Koch, a young Talmud student from Hungary. I had an argument with him the day before liberation. He said, "You'll see, G-d will hear you, He will save us", etc. To which I said, "So, so many are not heard. What right do I have to assume that G-d will save me? All I can say is – all I know is – I wouldn't deserve it, at least not fully". To that he had no answer. Then I myself came to this conclusion. I have to admit to myself that on strict justice I do not deserve to be saved by G-d. But I can equally grant G-d that He could let me survive, not through my desserts, but through His mercy. This I must also acknowledge. It would be blasphemous were I to regard G-d as a "justice-automat" (according to a human conception of justice). I may not presume upon it, but I acknowledge the possibility that He could allow His mercy to prevail. I cannot exclude this possibility, but I also cannot take it for granted.

I said, in a discussion with a Quaker group, that I somehow doubt whether one can at all speak *of* G-d and sometimes suspect that one – maybe – can only speak *to* G-d, that is, in the second – not the third – person. Then I said spontaneously, "Anyone who has ever stood in a concentration camp in a ditch with a pick and shovel and prayed there – has spoken *to* G-d – will doubt whether one can ever, at least in the same way and with the same inwardness, speak *of* G-d[17].

---

[15] Frankl himself was in Auschwitz.

[16] *Op. cit.*, p. 93

[17] This last paragraph is inserted from *ibid.*, pp. 96-97.

Education and self-transcendence[18]

Education should spur in young people the process of discovery of ethical purpose. Education should be concerned not simply to transmit knowledge, but also to hone the conscience of the young person: that one be sufficiently attuned as to be able to detect the ethical possibilities and imperatives of individual situations. How much more so, in an epoch in which for many the Ten Commandments seem to have lost their validity, must one be empowered to detect the ten thousand commandments (the thousand-fold application of the Ten Commandments) encoded in the ten thousand situations which confront one[19].

[As distinct from a spiritual education in objective values, we find that in a *secular* education] ethical purpose cannot be given. Indeed, meaning generally cannot be *given*, because meaning has to be found [through self-transcendence]. We cannot "prescribe" meaning. That is not the point or goal or task and it is also not possible. In principle, it is sufficient simply to stop blocking the process of discovery of meaning. The psychiatrist similarly does not have the task, we would argue, to give a person (who presently does not have it) the capacity to believe and to direct him or her to religion. It is enough that the psychiatrist stops preaching (the Freudian psychoanalytic dogma) that G-d is nothing but a father-image and religion nothing but the collective obsessional neurosis of humanity. And it would be already good, when pedagogues would stop serving up a model of the human being, that undermines the normal orientation to moral purpose – the idealism – which young people naturally possess.

For when I – whether as a student in an academic context, or as a psychological patient – am indoctrinated in pan-determinism, namely, that the human is no more than a product of heredity and environment or of conditioning processes, then one "rightly" says: I am not free and consequently I am not responsible. Why should I not commit criminal acts, why should I act morally?

---

[18] *Ibid.*, pp. 74-75.

[19] Frankl here distinguishes religious education from secular education, just as he distinguishes the psychiatrist's role from that of the religious mentor. This does not mean that religious education or mentoring should be absent from a person's life or education, but that secular education and psychotherapy, which operates in a secular milieu with people who are not necessarily religiously conscious, should *simply not block* the quest for ethical meaning. His point is that the "secular" individual – in education or psychotherapy – should be "drawn" through the process of self-transcendence to the discovery of objective meaning, rather than being lectured about it. For the secular individual, only a self-undertaken opening to meaning will be practical and effective.

When people are persuaded that the human is no more than a "naked ape", or they are persuaded that the human is the mere reflex of drives, or is no more than a product of the economic relations of production [as in Marxist ideology] or the product of conditioning learning processes – these indoctrinators have undermined the innate human orientation to ethical purpose.

In this way, the normal idealism and altruism of young people are systematically undermined. The great danger occurs when, from the outset, I regard people as "poor sausages" – as though "one's 'I' is not master in one's own house", as Freud says, or that one is no more than a reflex of conditioning, "beyond freedom and dignity", as Skinner puts it. Then I make the person worse than he or she is. I corrupt the person. If, on the other hand, I take the person as he or she ought to be, I make the person what he or she can become. I mobilize his or her authentic human potential.

The healthy soul in the sickest person[20]

You say that G-d is so great, that He can lower and make Himself small enough to slip into the most wretched person. Maybe you know this story from a book of mine. I tell of a patient who suffered from early childhood schizophrenia and who presented to me with uninterrupted hallucination and occasional deep agitation. I asked him, "How are you able to keep yourself together – as your sister told me you can – despite your distress?". He answered me after long hesitation, "I do it for G-d". Then it dawned on me what Kierkegaard meant when he said, "Even when madness offers me its fool's raiment, I can cling until the last the moment to my G-d". This non-determinedness! I have seen the worst psychic disorders – people lying in their excrement in wet straw, as it was in Zwokarna, as a section of the concentration camp Theresienstadt was named. A girl was there, whom I had known from Vienna and who was in effect a prostitute of the SS. There, in Theresienstadt, her manic depression broke out again and, in the last hours before her death, amidst manic episodes and exhaustion, she incessantly begged me to forgive her. I didn't know for what. And then I observed her just before her death – it was a scene like Gretchen in the first part of *Faust* – squat in the filthy

---

[20] *Ibid.*, p. 86.

straw and recite *Shema Yisrael*[21]. That, in the midst of a deep psychotic illness. That is what I mean by G-d slipping into the most wretched person.

The act of belief[22]

This brings me to introduce my definition of belief and I want to tell you how I came to it. When I was a child, we always heard in school that believing is the same as not-knowing, and not-knowing means being a donkey. That is to say, belief was portrayed as the minus-variant of thinking. I think the very opposite is the truth. I do not think that belief is a form of thinking, a mental act, which has a diminished[, an inferior] reality. To the contrary, belief is thinking, which gains in reality through the existential position of the one thinking it. This certainly does not mean that belief is not-knowing. Rather it means really that the act of believing is founded on an existential act. Blaise Pascal expressed the wager, or logical indeterminacy, of belief as follows. I can never *know* (logically) whether there is an ultimate meaning (G-d). Logically one can argue equally for either possibility. For reason, both are possibilities; neither possibility is compelled by reason. In other words, the scales stand equally balanced, both are equally possible. In this situation, a person has to decide, to say a *fiat*[23]; an Amen; a "so-is-it" – I do not know, but commit myself to it; or ... this is how I am going to act, so shall I live (namely) as though there were indeed an ultimate meaning; I am going to live as though there is a G-d. I throw my whole being into the scales, I allow my existence to speak, I declare my *fiat*, and that's it. I will act "as though..." it were – and thereby I make it – true; I raise myself up to be in its employ.

It is therefore not as a result of logical reasoning – because it cannot be out of mere lines of logical reasoning – that one comes to this decision. Rather one comes to this decision out of the depths of one's own being. Taking up *this* possibility of thought is both that – and more than – merely taking up the possibility. It makes *real* what was only a *possibility* for thought.

---

[21] "Hear O Israel [the L-rd our G-d, the L-rd is one]", the most basic Jewish prayer relating to the unity of G-d.

[22] *Op. cit.*, pp. 92-93.

[23] A decree, from the Latin, meaning "let it be (done)".

The practical ethical imperative[24]

One of my fundamental thoughts, which has emerged in the course of decades, occurred to me already as a fifteen year-old. It is the idea that we should not ask about the purpose of life; we cannot ask about it. There is a simple reason for this. We truly need to understand ourselves – our entire existence, our life – as something to which a question is *put*. We are the ones who are asked. It is *life*, which asks us. It is life, that places us before life's questions – which we have to answer. This answering is an answering for which we are responsible. That means, we answer the question about the purpose of life, in that we take responsibility for our lives. We cannot answer it with words, but ultimately only in deed.

---

[24] *G-ttsuche und Sinnfrage*, p. 119.

THE UNCONDITIONED HUMAN

Translated by Shimon Cowen

The physical is the condition, but not the cause of the mental and spiritual [faculties of the human being]. Physical sickness limits the expressive possibilities of the spiritual person, and physical treatment may restore them; that is to say, physical treatment gives the soul again the opportunity to express itself. This is all that clinical practice teaches us. All clinical practice can *explain* is the limitation of the possibilities of the human spirit. Understanding the reality of the spiritual is possible only from a meta-clinical standpoint.

There is some short-circuited thinking in the statement of a publication of an American writer: "Thyroid secretion increases the intelligence of subnormally intelligent people. Toxins disturb intellectual functions. What does this teach us? It shows that intellect is a natural material phenomenon. Or is it a kind of radiative emanation [of that material]?" Here the thyroid hormone is simply equated with spirit, a gross identification. The only thing missing here would be to assume, on the basis of our experience of electro-convulsive therapy with psychoses, that the human spirit can be equated with an electric current. In truth the current has obviously nothing to do with the human spirit – the one has nothing to do with the other, no connection with it. But let us ask quite generally, Who or what is receiving the shock in electroconvulsive therapy? Certainly not the spiritual person. Much rather, it is only the physical organism. Is it not high time that we ultimately face the question of what these two have to do with each other?

Over and again we have heard that the different ontological levels [of the person – body, mind and soul –] have to be kept rigorously distinct. In view of their distinctness we must refrain from conceptually confusing them. Yet the separate levels must somehow stand in some kind of describable relation to one another?

Indeed, this is the very case. The relationship between the spiritual person and the physical organism *is an instrumental one. The spirit instrumentalizes the psychophysical. The spiritual person organizes the psychophysical organism.* The former makes the latter its own, in that it makes it into an "Organon", an instrument.

It comes out then that the spiritual person relates to his or her organism analogously to the way a musician relates to a musical instrument. A sonata cannot be played without a piano or without a pianist. This metaphor explains a good deal – almost everything. But like every metaphor, this one too is deficient in some respect. For one can see the pianist [the player, analogous to the human soul], whereas the soul, as we have already heard, is *essentially* invisible (without thereby being unreal). That our analogy falters here has to do with the fact that pianist as well as the piano stand on the same level – literally: both on the same podium. The spirit and the body by no means find themselves on the same ontic level.

Notwithstanding all these shortcomings, we still consider the chosen comparison fruitful. Let us hold to it. On a mistuned piano the best pianist cannot play well (an analogy of illness). One then fetches the piano tuner (the therapeutic intervention), and he or she retunes the piano. Who would claim that the tuning of the piano establishes the pianist's artistry? We know that it cannot even make good the mistakes of a bad pianist...

How is it then, when it is not a piano, not the instrument of a pianist, but rather a person, who is "out of tune" – "out of tune", namely in the sense of an endogenous [bodily caused] state of discord. Consider the case of depression – not "reactive", not a mentally caused depression, but rather a somatic psychic illness, that is to say, a psychosis. Now we know already that psychosis is essentially something somatic, not a sickening of the authentic spirit, of the spiritual person. By no means is the spiritual person "afflicted" by depression, though there is no doubt that it "suffers under" the depression. Only the psychophysical organism can become sick and be sick. It is that which affected and afflicted by the depression. Once more it is evident here too that it is only the instrument that is out of tune – "instrument" and "out of tune" both literally [in the case of the piano] and metaphorically taken [in the case of the patient].

Now we understand. The therapist with the electro-convulsive apparatus corresponds thoroughly to the piano tuner. The mission of the one is like that of the other. The task and function of the therapist, just like the piano-tuner, has to do with restoration, resetting and repair of an apparatus. All that means is that the illness, like its treatment, applies exclusively to the apparatus, the instrument: both to becoming sick with a depression – as so-called psychosis, somatics – just like the electro-convulsive treatment – and the somatic therapy. The treatment gives the player [the patient] on this instrument [his or her unwell psychophysical organism], the ability to play, which the sickness had limited. As far as the [essential] person itself is concerned, this is as little affected by the depression as by its treatment. Neither the somatic illness nor the somatic treatment approach the spiritual person. The spiritual person is not affected by depression; the electro-convulsive electrodes are not applied to the spiritual person.

Where it is not a matter of psychotherapy in the sense of logotherapy and existential analysis, that is to say a therapy directed at the spiritual concept (Logos) and the spiritual subject (the existential person), but rather of a psychiatric therapy of psychotic processes (somatic treatment of somatic problems) [we have something else]. Notwithstanding fashionable theory, we are treating illnesses, but not ill *persons* themselves. For where we no longer treat sicknesses, but rather sick people as such – as people, as spiritual persons – it is not appropriate to speak of illness. There, the nosological [disease-classificatory] categories fall away, and there – in the realm of the personal spirit – only noological [meaning] categories are available. The categories are, however, no longer "healthy-sick", but rather "true-false".

Through an electrical shock, a depressive does not receive a new joy in living – as little as through secretion of the thyroid gland, new intellectual powers flow through to, and are incorporated in a person of hypothyroid-related subnormal intelligence. To say so, would be a bad materialist-energetics mistake. Just as the psychosis as such, that is, the somatic condition, which it ultimately presents, cannot be ascribed to the spiritual person, so also the personal spirit (which becomes effective again after successful treatment of the psychophysical-organic sickness) does not itself pertain to somatic therapy.

"The spiritual person" remains untouched even in the state of psychosis; the personal spirit is not broached by the "mental illness". However much the [essential] person may be obscured and hidden by a foreground illness, it continues to stand in the background as before, albeit [presently] powerless and invisible: "powerless" in terms of the use of the instrument which was made for it, namely the psychophysical organism; "invisible" in all but individual moments in which the soul, like a flash of lightning, breaks through the psychophysical layer isolating it from us[1].

This psychophysical entity – not the soul – is sick. This cannot be sufficiently emphasized. For one who ascribes psychosis not to the psychophysical, but locates it in the essential person, denies the mentally ill person his or her essential humanity; and moreover conflicts with the therapeutic ethic. [With this view] the treating therapist will no longer see sufficient grounds for proceeding with the therapeutic [restorative] intervention. For the therapeutic intervention presumes a "something" for the sake of which it is pursued. Better said, it presumes not a something but a someone, that is, an existing person, pre- and post-sickness. For a mere "something", a mere organism, it is possible that no one would be a healer. One can want to be a healer only for the person, who "bears" the particular, diseased organism. One can want to be a healer only for a person, who "is" not sick, but "has" a sickness. I treat "concerning" an illness, but "for the sake of" a person. I treat not for the sake of the organism, but rather I treat their organism for the sake of the person. (Not even a veterinarian treats an animal for the sake of the animal organism. He or she too treats it for the sake of a person, for the sake of the one, to whom the animal belongs).

Psychosis is a somatic phenomenon. It is the psychic manifestation of a somatic illness. As such it is the sickening of a psychophysical organism, but not of the spiritual person. The spiritual person is simply "walled in" by [the sick psychophysical organism]. Who then, if not the therapist, should be the one positioned to sense the person behind this wall, the suffering person? The [essential] person, as mentioned, "suffers under" the psychosis, without itself being sickened [by the psychosis]. The person suffers simply under the powerlessness, to which it has been condemned by the psychosis – namely, under a powerlessness to manifest itself. For to manifest itself, the person needs an organism which functions undisturbed both as instrument and expression [of the essential person]...

The soul reveals itself as indeed not totally determined by the physical; not as total limitation, but rather as a residual freedom of the spirit. This is the relative independence of the soul, or in the words of Nicolai Hartmann

---

[1] The term "powerless" relates to the instrumental relationship of the spiritual to the bodily. To what does the term "invisible" relate? In fact, the relationship of the essential person to the organism is not only an instrumental, but also a [self-]expressive one. Where the spiritual person can no longer *express* itself in any, or at least in an undisturbed functioning organism, then it becomes *invisible*.

"Autonomy despite dependency". To this I add: we see so much, more than enough, that the task remains to trace that residual freedom of the spirit in existential-analytic practice, in order to appeal to it logotherapeutically. At the same time, the positive aspect of this freedom should never be forgotten. This is the responsibility – the "to where" – of this freedom, as the counterpart of the "from where" [of negative freedom].

Why did we draw the inference just now that freedom to spirituality is – in clinical terms – an inference *"per exclusionem"* [conclusion through progressive rejection of other possible explanations]? It is evident everywhere that under the same psychophysical conditions the spiritual [response], which might be imagined to be influenced by these conditions themselves, in varying circumstances in fact differs. This spiritual power must therefore be an unconditioned one. The spiritual reality cannot be a *totally* conditioned one. Rather it is an influencing reality. The spiritual reality is itself [the power] of influence.

We have elsewhere noted that the same psychophysical manifestation of illness, which we called endogenous depression with melancholia *[endogene Melancholie]*, whether in its somatic or psychological features, allows the most varying spiritual responses. That is to say, the spiritual person as the one who bears the unwell psychophysical organism, permits and makes possible these different stances towards [the unwell organism] to the extent that [the organism] allows it – the [essential] person – that scope. We shall encounter this scope when we come to speak about psychiatric genetics. This scope is evident in every place which is left free of conditioning elements, which is filled with the non-conditioned. Accordingly, the human manifests him or herself – in the realm of this free scope for spiritual stances – as undetermined, at least as far as possibility allows. The human being is factually conditioned but facultatively unconditioned.

Precisely the brain pathologist and the specialist in psychiatric genetics are the ones who know about these limitations which spiritual freedom experiences through psychophysical illness. Yet, exactly these experts on psychophysical conditioning factors at the same time always become witnesses – witnesses of spiritual freedom, witnesses of that free scope which leads *per exclusionem* to the inference of a power over psychophysical conditions, a spiritual freedom. What is revealed to these witnesses is the power of the spiritual person, in the midst of, and in spite of, all seeming powerlessness. I would like to put it this way: that which presents itself to them as such is the defiant power of the human spirit.

Does not the piano-tuner have an opportunity to marvel at the virtuoso who can play better on an untuned piano, than a bad player does on a good piano? [The great philosopher] Kant [in old age] had the use of no more than a brain in a condition of *status cribrosus* [a condition marked by dilations of the perivascular spaces in the brain]. In the last days of his life, he exhibited a severe amnestic aphasic condition [– an inability to name objects or recognize objects by their names –] but what words were drawn from this "instrument"! His doctors wanted him for a meeting to discuss his medical case and[, when it eventuated,] waited long – in vain – for him to sit down. Eventually, they understood that their patient had refused to take his seat so long as the doctors themselves had not sat. Once they did, Kant wrestled from his atherosclerotic brain the profoundly moving words: "I have not yet lost my sense of humanity". Behold: a virtuoso plays on a bad instrument.

Let us sum up. The physical body [the flesh] is a mere possibility. As such it is open to something which could realize this possibility. For, in itself, the physical possibility is no more or less than the blank form, prepared by the biological base, which awaits a filling out. Thus, not only is the somatic [– the bodily –] open to the psyche [– the mental –], but the psychic is also open to the spiritual. The task of the scientist is to preserve this openness. The sciences of the physical and mental – the physical and mental conditioners of the human – i.e. biology and psychology respectively have to keep the doors open – those doors which literally lead out of this double determinedness into freedom, into the realm of the spiritual. Science has to keep these doors open, but at the same time, the scientist must not venture far beyond these doors. He or she may not plant him- or herself in a realm not theirs – for example in the supernatural realm. It could easily happen that the unwatched doors could shut behind him [and that he would have exceeded, and thereby vitiated the competence in that area which he or she had].

Science can do no more than deliver such material as can, without contradiction, be built into a theistic world-view. Their job is not to build it in to that world-view, but rather that is the job of other builders.

Let us return to our argument, according to which the bodily dimension (as mere possibility-conferring) needs the mental dimension (as its realization) and finally the spiritual dimension as its [– the mental dimension's –] fulfilment. We could couch this double relation, in the following terms – in a conditional clause and a causal clause: when something is physically possible, it is made real through the mental, because it is a spiritual necessity.

To make this clear, let us use our metaphor of the piano one last time. Does the piano play? No. It merely makes a performance possible. Does the pianist play simply because he or she can? No. It is rather because he or she must play. In the performance he or she "brings out" the "possibilities" of the instrument according to artistic necessity. Precisely that is the relationship between the ontic levels (in the human being): the physical makes possible the mental realization of a spiritual demand.